Endowment
Essentials for Museums

Endowment Essentials for Museums

Rebekah Beaulieu

ROWMAN & LITTLEFIELD
Lanham • Boulder • New York • London

Published by Rowman & Littlefield
An imprint of The Rowman & Littlefield Publishing Group, Inc.
4501 Forbes Boulevard, Suite 200, Lanham, Maryland 20706
www.rowman.com

86-90 Paul Street, London EC2A 4NE

British Library Cataloguing in Publication Information Available

Library of Congress Cataloging-in-Publication Data

Names: Beaulieu, Rebekah, author. | American Association for State and
  Local History.
Title: Endowment essentials for museums / Rebekah Beaulieu.
Description: Lanham : Rowman & Littlefield, [2022] | Series: American
  Association for State and Local History book series | Includes
  bibliographical references and index.
Identifiers: LCCN 2022006430 (print) | LCCN 2022006431 (ebook) | ISBN
  9781538128091 (cloth) | ISBN 9781538128107 (paperback) | ISBN
  9781538128114 (ebook)
Subjects: LCSH: Museum finance. | Museums—Accounting. | Museums—Planning.
Classification: LCC AM122 .B39 2022 (print) | LCC AM122 (ebook) | DDC
  069.068/1—dc23/eng/20220223
LC record available at https://lccn.loc.gov/2022006430
LC ebook record available at https://lccn.loc.gov/2022006431

Contents

Acknowledgments

This publication simply would not have been possible without the guidance, support, and expertise of so many. I wish to thank Charles Harmon of Rowman & Littlefield, whose early confidence in and encouragement of the project was instrumental in my taking on a topic as monumental as endowments, especially so soon after the publication of *Financial Fundamentals for Historic House Museums*. The entire Rowman & Littlefield team is responsive, knowledgeable, and a delight. Thank you for all of your help as I made progress, sometimes slower than I would have liked!

One of the benefits of this project was the opportunity it provided to work with Michelle Beckett once more, an absolutely incredible—and very entertaining!—editor. Every time I send Michelle a project for review, I feel a sense of joyful anticipation: not only to be able to turn over my messy drafts, ripe for editing, but also in anticipation of whatever humorous asides she will incorporate into her recommendations.

I deeply appreciate the contributions of time and candor that my museum colleagues have offered to me as I worked on this publication over the past four years and, most of all, to those who agreed to have their sites profiled as case studies for each chapter: Dawn Salerno of the Rotch-Jones-Duff House and Garden Museum; Vivian Zoë of the Slater Museum at the Norwich Free Academy; Erin Branham of the Los Angeles County Museum of Art; Sarah George of the University of Utah and formerly of the Natural History Museum of Utah; Joshua Torrance, now at the Webb-Deane-Stevens Museum and formerly of the Woodlawn Museums, Gardens & Park; Neil Gordon of the Discovery Museum; Phelan Fretz of ECHO, Leahy Center for Lake Champlain; Larry Yerdon of Strawbery Banke; Colleen Schafroth of the Maryhill Museum of Art; and Julia Marciari-Alexander of the Walters Art Museum.

Finally, I would be remiss not to thank the wonderful professional and personal community with whom I am so fortunate to share each day. The staff of the Florence Griswold Museum is a team to which I am honored to contribute, and I owe a particular note of gratitude to my assistant, Melissa Díaz, who is truly essential in making sure I am able to find time for all my crazy projects. Matthew Strekel, Director of Development, was a welcome sounding board and contributor to discussions of procedures and protocol. I am lucky to work with a group of professionals who make me think and laugh every single day.

To Jerry and Julie Ford, I thank you for your consistent support and inspiration to always stay curious. To Dan and Debbie Beaulieu, thank you for always encouraging me to think outside the box and find ways to foster my passion for my work. And to my husband, Patrick Ford, thank you for each and every day together, and for being the best partner a museum-obsessed gal could ever have.

Preface

You enter a museum for the first time. Perhaps it is an opulent structure, an icon of artistry and rich in collections of fine art and artifacts amassed over centuries, an institution that attracts visitors from around the globe. Or maybe it is a site on a more intimate scale, a local historical society or small art museum with relatively modest exhibitions and collections, but priceless to the cultural fabric of a community. Before you peruse thoughtfully curated exhibitions, announcements of educational programs, and tours, you walk up to a massive visitor reception area—or simply to the volunteer docents who await you with a smile—and you say: "Show me your investment policy."

Sounds like a stickup, doesn't it?

For virtually all of us who work in, volunteer time to, and enjoy museums, endowments are not the first things we notice when we cross their thresholds. We expect to engage with history, science, and art—to be welcomed to an environment of learning. Our interest in museums is fostered via their work on behalf of and to the public, their relationship to their communities, and their adherence to their missions. Yet just as invaluable to an organization as its public persona is how its financial resources are managed. The function of museums as accountable to the public trust ensures that we should endeavor to govern and administer sites to ensure their vitality for years to come.

The topic of nonprofit endowments is often discussed in terms of institutions of higher education, due in large part to their prominence and size. In 2018, the largest educational endowments were those of Harvard University ($39 billion), Yale University ($29 billion), and Stanford University ($26 billion).[1] Higher education endowments have been in the spotlight since 2009, when the Great Recession negatively impacted the stock market. Legislation has countered the ever-growing endowments of large private universities with regulations such as the Tax Cuts and Jobs Act of 2017 and the Bipartisan Budget Act of 2018, which levies a 1.4 percent excise tax on "investment returns at private colleges with at least 500 students whose endowments are valued at more than $500,000 per student."[2] Though such a tax applies to only approximately thirty-five institutions of higher education in the Unites States and was intended to create a sense of parity between highly funded schools and others, the measure was unpopular for its redistribution of funds from student aid and scholarships to taxation of nonprofits. The Treasury Department and Internal Revenue Service later revised the rule to discount those students whose tuitions are paid through federal grants, and the endowment tax is still under review by both agencies.[3] While legislation and the press focus on the astronomical value of endowments in one sector of nonprofit industry, it begs the question: What about the rest of us not in higher education and without multibillion dollar investments?

While the topic of higher education endowments makes headlines, that of museum endowments has maintained a lower profile—but not always. Museum endowments have been a hot button issue in the popular press over the past decade, and heightened attention is paid to museum investments in light of recent discussions regarding deaccessioning.[4] While a buzz has existed about endowments and their part in strengthening—or weakening—a museum, virtually no literature exists that provides an in-depth discussion of endowments from a professional perspective.

Until now, endowments have been addressed only perfunctorily. Management texts such as *Streetsmart Financial Basics for Nonprofit Managers* by Thomas A. McLaughlin, *Slaying the Financial Dragon: Strategies for Museums* by the American Association of Museums, *Thriving in the Knowledge Age: New Business Models for Museums and Other Cultural Institutions* by John H. Falk and Beverly K. Sheppard, *The Manual of Strategic Planning for Cultural Institutions* by Gail Dexter Lord and Kate Markert, and *The Legal Guide for Museum Professionals* edited by Julia Courtney are all excellent references for those interested in museum finance and compliance, but all devote minor attention to endowments and usually only to caution against overreliance on endowment funds and the potential strings attached. Similarly, books that speak on the topic of fundraising, like Karen Brooks Hopkins and Carolyn Stolper Friedman's *Successful Fundraising for Arts and Cultural Organizations*, Sarah S. Brophy's *Is Your Museum Grant-Ready?: Assessing Your Organization's Potential for Funding*, Salvatore G. Cilella Jr.'s *Fundraising for Small Museums: In Good Times and Bad*, Cinnamon Catlin-Legutko and Stacy Klingler's *Small Museum Toolkit 2: Financial Resource Development and Management*, and Juilee Decker's *Fundraising and Strategic Planning* speak about endowments as part of the institutional planning process without providing details regarding fund establishment, management, cultivation, and evaluation. Deborah Kaplan Polivy's *The Time for Endowment Building Is Now* is a fantastic resource regarding endowments in the context of fundraising and geared toward those fundraisers comfortable with the topic. These colleagues in the museum field have done remarkable work in the creation of resources for those eager to tackle strong management principles, but there exists a void when it comes to introductory texts about endowments.

The creation and management of endowment funds is not sexy. Nope. It is hard work and often requires museum professionals to stretch beyond the interests that originally attracted them to the field, and it requires investment and finance committee service that we ask of our most dedicated trustees. When most people who work in museums are asked whether they would like to spend their day revising an investment policy or discussing a new acquisition to the collection, they're pretty sure they know which activity would win. Many of us in the museum community have avoided financial topics altogether, cobbling together a basic understanding of income and expenses and operating budgets while leaving more sophisticated topic to others.

This book is the first of its kind to offer a foundation for understanding endowment structures and functions for those of us in the museum profession. It addresses how to handle internal endowment management, external relations with stakeholders, and compliance standards. Chapter 1 lays the groundwork for comprehending museum terminology and introduces the history, language, and structures of endowments. The second chapter is dedicated to the role of the board in governing endowments and the policies recommended for strong financial oversight. Chapter 3 provides a discussion of endowments in terms of financial management and accounting principles, and chapter 4 focuses on endowments and fundraising. Transparency is the focus of chapter 5, which details the annual reporting process and mission-relevant endowment management. Each chapter includes issues in the field that identify topics of interest to museum endowments, and case studies chronicle a variety of budget sizes, content areas, geographical location, and maturity to highlight a variety of institutional approaches to endowments.

This book is designed for museum professionals, volunteers, and trustees of all backgrounds and at every comfort level with financial topics. Additionally, it is a resource for institutions of all sizes, content areas, and locations, from volunteer-run sites who are just getting started thinking about endowment establishment to established organizations with decades-old funds. There are no prerequisites to the education provided in this publication; it is designed to be accessible, inviting, and to encourage you to learn more about a system of asset management that could substantially benefit your organization.

Many of us are less than totally comfortable with financial conversations, and this book will equip you with a basic understanding of endowments and their value for financial and planning purposes, as well as the role endowments can serve in discussions with community members and prospective donors. We often hear endowment horror stories or criticism of extremely high-value endowments, which are certainly not representative of the field. The reality is that endowments are appropriate and relevant to organizations of all sizes and can play a vital part in the future viability of your organization.

What is this book *not* intended to do? To scold, criticize, or dismiss those who are unfamiliar with financial matters. Perhaps you are a newly minted director or trustee recognizing that endowments are something you finally need to tackle. Or a student in an undergraduate or graduate program who dreams of working in museums, eager to be an attractive candidate when you enter the job market. If you are willing to learn, this resource is for you.

Above all else, this book is designed to help us have meaningful conversations about museum endowments. So let's start talking.

NOTES

1. Investopedia, "Endowment," by Tim Smith, last updated April 27, 2020, https://www.investopedia.com/terms/e/endowment.asp.
2. Paul Oliveira, "New College Endowment Tax Under the Tax Cuts and Jobs Act," Kahn, Litwin, Renza (blog), September 5, 2018, https://kahnlitwin.com/blogs/tax-blog/new-college-endowment-tax-under-the-tax-cuts-and-jobs-act.
3. Kery Murakami, "Treasury Modifies Endowment Tax Rules," Inside Higher Ed, September 21, 2020, https://www.insidehighered.com/quicktakes/2020/09/21/treasury-modifies-endowment-tax-rules.
4. See Judith Dobrzynski, "How an Acquisition Fund Burnishes Reputations," *New York Times*, March 14, 2012; Gareth Harris, "Museums Are Wising up to the Benefits of Endowment Funds," *Museums Journal* (2015), https://www.museumsassociation.org/museums-journal/analysis/2014/12/02012015-museums-wising-up-endowment-funds/; and "Berkshire Museum Sanctioned for Selling Artworks to Boost Endowment" *Philanthropy News Digest*, June 1, 2018, https://philanthropynewsdigest.org/news/berkshire-museum-sanctioned-for-selling-artworks-to-boost-endowment.

1

Start on the Right Foot

UNDERSTANDING THE BASICS OF THE ENDOWMENT

The endowment serves a fundamental purpose in the health of an organization, and it is of the utmost importance to understand its essential components and management. Let's start with the basics.

WHAT IS AN ENDOWMENT?

An endowment is a donation of money or property that can be sold for monetary value to a nonprofit organization, which uses the income from said gift for a specific purpose. This purpose may be general (unrestricted) or for a defined project or need (restricted). The term *endowment* can refer to a single fund or donor gift, or a group or number of funds. More colloquially, it typically refers to the totality of a nonprofit institution's investable assets. Endowment funds are invested for a period of time as defined when the endowment is established, typically in perpetuity.

HOW DOES THE ENDOWMENT RELATE TO ORGANIZATIONAL MISSION?

An endowment is not required by law for nonprofit organizations, and many do not have one. Organizations that are particularly reliant on earned revenue—such as private event rentals, for instance—and with minimal operational expenses may rely less on contributed income and invested funds. Such arrangements do not necessarily support a mission, which could ultimately compromise tax exempt status; of equal significance, they do not allow for sustainable income to be generated from institutional investments instead of external sources. As we will discuss more specifically in later chapters, the endowment allows for nuanced management that is focused on understanding regular operational needs as well as to prepare for times of institutional transition, growth, and challenge.

The ultimate purpose of the endowment is to create a fund for extended, strategic use to benefit the organization in the long run. It demonstrates an organization's investment in its future and commitment to long-term planning. Once an endowment has been established, it provides essential funding to the typical operations of the organization, which in turn allows the organization to perform its stated mission. Furthermore, the provision of perpetual income can relieve pressure on short-term fundraising efforts that result in one-time gifts, and create a financial system that allows for independence and fortitude. An endowment can also build a welcoming structure of future giving from a donor base for years to come.

The external optics of a well-managed endowment cannot be overstated. The endowment allows the opportunity for donors to invest in the future of an organization, and to make a meaningful contribution that benefits the organization immediately and in the longer term. As donors age and their philanthropic considerations turn to lifetime giving plans and potential future bequests, the endowment offers a place to direct their gifts that will make a lasting impact. A bequest to the endowment can symbolize a dedication to sound financial practice, fiscal sustainability, and oversight, especially for those donors who have served as trustees or have a particular interest in the financial health of the organization. For others, it may serve as a way to structure a giving plan over time, with the ability to make regular gifts over a period of years with the assurance that these gifts will support the essential and mission-based functions of the organization. The endowment is unmatched in its ability to reinforce a commitment to organizational sustainability, mission-specific activities, and donor relations.

HISTORICAL PERSPECTIVES ON THE ENDOWMENT

We understand the modern endowment as a means to maintain institutional and donor confidence. But where did endowments come from and how did we come to rely on them? Let's take a moment to learn about the evolution of the endowment, which allows us a quick breather from financial management and a chance for a brief history lesson!

The first endowments were founded by Marcus Aurelius in Greece, circa 176 CE, as part of his commitment to and establishment of education in the country's capital of Athens. The first funds were established to support professorships to chair each of the four traditional schools of thought.[1] The practice continued throughout the history of Western education—notably, in the creation of endowed professorships in England by King Henry VIII and his descendants, the oldest of which are endowed chairs in the Faculty of Divinity at the University of Cambridge and still active today.[2] These early examples demonstrate the initial purpose of endowments: to serve schools and to create in perpetuity funding for specific purposes. Much of this resonates in how we define endowments today.

But what about our modern understanding of endowments for institutional purposes? The modern American use of endowments dates to the late 1920s, when a public conversation commenced with a focus on the differences between a charitable trust, its use defined only for a specific period, versus a perpetual and permanently held endowment. It is no surprise, by the way, that such topics were under scrutiny after the establishment of the first estate tax as part of the Revenue Act of 1916 and in light of the stock market crash in 1929. Discernment between the two had never been considered in American philanthropy; the earliest activity was the establishment of colleges during the colonial period. Documentation of this debate was published in a 1929 piece for *Atlantic Monthly* by Julius Rosenwald, a founder of Sears, Roebuck & Co., titled "The Principles of Public Giving."[3] In this article, Rosenwald encouraged other major philanthropists to create foundations by which to support causes, and with a finite end to "sunset" their giving before death to avoid the posthumous estate tax on their fortunes.

The estate tax and the Great Depression served to reset the American understanding of the role and purpose of endowments, which had long gone under-researched and unquestioned. At the time, many criticized the seeming stagnancy of endowments. In a 1997 article for the *Arizona Law Review*, Evelyn Brody argues that the general distaste for endowments was also in protest against the increasing concentration of wealth in the endowments of elite colleges and universities.[4] Indeed, this is a topic that maintains notoriety in our current debates on endowments.

While the centralization of endowments in the coffers of elite institutions of higher education remains a thorn in the side of many donors and nonprofit professionals, they also skew the general perception of the value of endowments for organizations of all sizes. The twenty-first century has ushered in a renewed appreciation for endowments, as nonprofits—particularly in the cultural sector—attend more fully to sound business practices and an increasing understanding of financial best practices. The utility of endowments as a vital asset base, funding and stewardship opportunity for sustained donor relationships, and perpetual funding source is vital to many organizations in this new economic landscape. Corrections to the stock market due to overly dynamic fluctuations in the 2000s, the 2009 recession, and the economic fallout from the 2020 coronavirus pandemic all highlight the reliance on endowments as a necessity during turbulent economic circumstances.

THE STRUCTURE AND CLASSIFICATIONS OF ENDOWMENTS

Now that we have a common understanding of the history of endowments, you may question why they receive so much attention. What makes them both so desirable and controversial at the same time? Much of that has to do with their structure, which is actually quite straightforward.

The endowment comprises two components: the principal and the income. The principal, also known as the corpus, is the amount of the original investment, which is to remain untouched in order to allow the monies to accrue value. Since a single endowment may consist of one gift from a single donor, multiple gifts from a single donor, or multiple gifts from multiple donors, the principal should be calculated to account for the principal amounts of all gifts included in the fund. The income is the amount of appreciation that exceeds the principal and is available for current use. A portion of this appreciated value, also referred to as the distribution or draw, is a percentage earned from the investment. The rate of distribution should be documented and approved by the governing board of the organization, and any revisions or exceptions to the income similarly recorded. This structure is quintessential to the endowment and defined by the principal investment and the earnings generated. However, the endowment is also uniquely characterized by its timeframe. Unlike gifts that are used in their entirety for a specific initiative—such as a campaign gift to assist with a capital project—endowment gifts are constructed so that the principal can be conserved and so that it will never be fully spent out, but maintained in perpetuity.[5] Consider this example: Let's say that a donor is interested in supporting acquisitions. If the donor writes a check to fund the purchase of a work of art, the gift would be processed accordingly and spent in full. If instead the donor decides to support an acquisition fund, the gift would be deposited into an investment account and the amount used for acquisitions limited to that which is distributed annually and according to the percentage predetermined by the board. In this case, the principal would remain untouched and the fund allowed to increase in value. The construction of an endowment follows these rules of form and time, though they can vary in terms of how they are to be managed.

Supplemental information also serves a fundamental role in the structure of the endowment, which will be explored in in the chapters to come. If an endowment gift is solicited via an ask and/or a structured campaign, a case statement should offer potential donors a description of the goals of the campaign and the potential use of the gift. This is especially useful when a formal campaign is structured to support an endowment campaign (see chapter 4).

One additional distinction for endowments is for those that are unrestricted and available for general operating use as opposed to those that carry donor restrictions, which may explicate legally binding guidelines according to use, timeline, and capacity. Below are some of the most commonly used endowment fund subtypes to help you distinguish between them for internal management purposes and the variety of donor restrictions that may be imposed.

General Endowment

The most basic form of endowment is the general endowment, which is designed to fund general operational needs. If you are considering establishing an endowment for an organization that has never before had an endowment (or to resuscitate a fund designed in the past to be an endowment but never quite got off the ground), a general operating endowment is a great place to start. General endowments provide the most benefit to the organization because they are generally *unrestricted*, meaning they are free from donor-imposed spending restrictions, and most attractive to those donors interested in investing in general organizational health and sustainability. The general endowment is usually an amalgamation of donations from multiple sources and forms as well as instrumental to the accommodation of general needs.

Named Funds

Named or honorific funds are those that are named for a specific donor or to honor an individual, family, or other entity. Named funds are often restricted in use according to guidelines, or terms, that are defined by the donor(s) when the fund is created. Named funds typically require a higher gift to establish the fund because the donor pool is small or single in source, as opposed to general endowments that are funded by a potentially large pool of funders. Like all endowments, the fund can be populated by gifts over multiple years. Until the goal of a certain amount is reached, it will be considered a pre-endowment fund. Many donors decide to establish an endowment, give an annual amount to build the fund gradually, and draft a bequest to fully fund the endowment in their estate plans. During the pre-endowment phase, funders can allow the fund to be used at their discretion before it is subject to spend restrictions according to the endowment distribution rate. For example, I have worked with a docent who was passionate about education programs and fell in love with a program we were trying to get off the ground. She requested that $10,000 be reallocated from her pre-endowment fund to support the program. This flexibility worked well because it allowed her the opportunity to directly support a program before endowment-specific restrictions were in place. The only downside was the reduction in the value of the pre-endowment fund and the additional time that would be necessary to reach the endowment threshold (though the donor's enthusiasm about new educational programs certainly built her confidence in her long-term philanthropic intentions).

Specific-Use Funds

Specific-use funds are exactly what they sound like: funds that are restricted for particular use, typically mission-direct activities such as educational programs, acquisitions, exhibitions, or conservation of the collection. These may be named for a specific individual, such as detailed in the section above, or may be funded by a group of funders. In whatever ways the fund is constructed, its purpose is specific and well-defined. Specific-use funds are popular for the chance they offer funders to support specific needs of the organization that would otherwise not be met or to fund staff positions that are integral to the institutional mission. Director and chief curator positions, for instance, are popular choices for endowed positions because if funded by endowment income, these positions are secure from any financial challenges an organization may face that would lead to dreaded downsizing. One consideration to keep in mind is that the uses for which endowment funds are secured should be in accordance with the core functions of the organization and with the expectation to continue in perpetuity.

Term Endowments

Term endowments are those restricted by the timeframe of their existence, whether defined by a particular period of time or upon the occurrence of a specific event. While most endowments are intended to exist in perpetuity, term endowments are those designated to function as endowments, with spending calculated as a percentage of the value of the fund, for only a specific period of time. Following the conclusion of the timeframe or event, the donor restrictions are retired and the remainder of the fund is to be used or invested at the discretion of the organization. Term endowments were much more common in the early days of modern institutional investments and less common than the other types of endowments mentioned.

It is important for your organization to offer a number of endowment-giving opportunities and the ability to create a fund according to donor preferences. In addition to the endowment fund subtypes explained above, we should take a moment to note that there are a variety of fund structures available to donors and how these are overseen.

True Endowment

A true endowment is one that can be limited in time or be held in perpetuity and used to fund general operations or a specific purpose. When we consider the endowment in its most essential form, it is a true endowment. A true endowment can be unrestricted for general use or restricted for a specific use, it may be named or unnamed, it may be funded by one donor or a collective of support. The bottom line is that its terms, timeline, and funding amount are determined by the donor.

Other Fund Types and Designations

Quasi endowments, on the other hand, are funds according to the discretion of the governing board of trustees, whether according to a particular schedule or for a specific use. They are also called board-restricted funds. Funds that are designated for particular purposes by a governing board, without restriction by the donor and considered quasi endowments, are regarded as unrestricted and can be reallocated without penalty and in compliance with the original gift. Additional restrictions placed on gifts for certain use—for example, an allocation from the general endowment for a capital project, acquisitions, strategic planning, publications, and so on—are internally managed and not subject to the stringent laws to which donor-restricted gifts are subject. Furthermore, keep in mind that boards can earmark monies for specific use that may be endowments (in which the principal should be reserved) or not (in which the entire amount can be spent). Quasi endowments can also refer to funds that have been raised for a certain use via a campaign effort, as a result of an operating revenue surplus, or from currently-held institutional funds, and refers to the definition of use by the board and not a donor.

Reserve funds are those that are available and ready for use. Their high liquidity makes them ideal for accommodating cash flow issues or to fund capital needs, technological upgrades, unforeseen expenses, or other costs that exceed budget expectations but are necessary expenditures. Many organizations populate a reserve fund from operating income surpluses, or for gifts to support particular purposes or via structured campaigns. Let's say that you have a building that needs a new roof and a donor offers to fund the expense. That gift would not be invested, but would be used for the immediate purpose. From a cash flow perspective, if you secured a grant to fund a roof replacement but the funds are not to be dispersed until after the replacement is needed, reserve funds could be used to fund the expense and the grant would then be used to replenish the fund.

* * * * *

CASE STUDY: THE ROTCH-JONES-DUFF HOUSE AND GARDEN MUSEUM NEW BEDFORD, MASSACHUSETTS

Mission: In addition to preserving and restoring the house, the Rotch-Jones-Duff House and Garden Museum strives to demonstrate New Bedford's place in the nation's history through educational programming and exhibits.

In 1834, William Rotch Jr. commissioned British-American architect Richard Upjohn to design a Greek Revival home, the first residential commission Upjohn received. Rotch was, for decades, a whaling merchant and the wealthiest man in New Bedford, a Quaker, and a staunch abolitionist in the Quaker tradition. Along with the homes, the Jones and Duff families, the inhabitants of the Rotch, James, and Duff homes are affiliated with the flourishing whaling industry of nineteenth-century New Bedford. The residences remained in private hands until 1981, when purchased along with extensive gardens by the preservationist group WHALE (the Waterfront Historic Area League) and transformed into a historic house museum. Today, the Rotch-Jones-Duff House is located in the center of the city's County Street Historical District, and the one-acre site is a popular destination for those interested in the history of New Bedford and the whaling economy, and its gardens are popular among garden enthusiasts.

According to longtime trustee and former treasurer Nathanael Brayton, the Board of Trustees of the Rotch-Jones-Duff House and Gardens Museum first considered the establishment of an endowment in the late 1990s, when the museum

Figure 1.1. The Rotch-Jones-Duff House and Garden Museum. Courtesy of the Rotch-Jones-Duff House and Gardens.

faced the imminent conclusion of an annual gift of $25,000, which had supported much of the museum's operations since its opening in 1981. The donor, a descendant of one of the namesake families, stipulated that his annual gift was to serve in lieu of a bequest, and had reached the age of ninety-three. The board of trustees knew it needed to plan for the funding transition and how to support the museum after the donor passed away. At that time, the Rotch-Jones-Duff Museum and Gardens' assets included no endowment but a reserve fund that amounted to a modest $150,000, equivalent to roughly five months of operating costs. The board of trustees was reluctant to use these funds to start an endowment, especially since it would not be nearly enough to provide sufficient operational support.

The museum faced extremely lean years of low revenue early in its existence, and its leadership knew that preparation for the future was essential, and the generation of funds to match or exceed the annual gift of $25,000 was vital to the museum's survival. The board of trustees also realized that the structure in which the donor had contributed his annual gift required little staff time investment, and that the most logical replacement would be that of an invested fund, which would provide sustainability while requiring little ongoing cultivation from the modestly sized staff. The board established a distribution rate policy of a 4 percent rate of spending that would distribute at least $25,000. With that in mind, the museum's board of trustees established an endowment campaign with an internal fundraising need of $625,000 and a publicized goal of $1 million, all to be raised from scratch.

The campaign was established. By the time the donor of the annual gift passed on, the museum had exceeded its internal need, its original external goal of $1 million, and even surpassed a revised goal of $1.25 million. The fund was officially opened in 2005. Today it holds a value of approximately $2.1 million and is distributed according to the 4 percent rate originally approved by the board of trustees in the 1990s. It remains a vital source of institutional operating support to this day.

What Can We Learn?

- *It is essential to plan beyond annual gifts that support essential functions.* Investment income is a sustainable complement to annual gifts that, due to economic climate or personal circumstance, can cease at any time.
- *Consider staff capacity when determining a funding structure.* The scrutiny of the board of trustees into the time investment to bring in gifts via the annual campaign versus the security of a regular investment distribution informed their decision.
- *Plan for more than you think you will need.* In this case, the museum's board of trustees set a higher fundraising goal than they knew they wound need to survive, which allowed for more stability and reduced the need for subsequent fundraising for the endowment.

In the case of the Rotch-Jones-Duff Museum and Gardens, the board of trustees recognized the need to keep their reserve fund available for short-term needs and to build their endowment from the ground up. Many organizations consider a reserve fund and an endowment virtually indistinguishable, which is certainly not the case. A reserve fund should always be tapped, especially for emergency use, before an endowment. Furthermore, a reserve fund is liquid and easily accessible, while the endowment is invested. Unlike the reserve fund, the endowment is only to be used according to the distribution rate. A reserve fund is *not* a replacement for an endowment, and ideally an organization should diversify between funds that may be highly liquid but low interest generating (reserve funds) and those that are not liquid but with high earning potential (endowments). They are used for different purposes and managed according to different standards and best practices. Look at it this way: you wouldn't place your entire retirement fund in a savings account, and you most likely wouldn't access your 401(k) to pay for an unforeseen house expense. Reserve and endowment funds function similarly (which is to say they function differently).

* * * * *

ISSUES IN THE FIELD:
TO HAVE AN ENDOWMENT OR NOT: AN ARGUMENT
FOR THE ENDOWMENT

Now that the basic structure and function of the endowment has been introduced, you may still wonder if an endowment is the right choice for your organization, and understandably so. This is an ongoing debate in the museum field. Unlike other fundraising efforts that yield results for immediate use, the establishment of an endowment fund takes time, often years, and with a relatively modest return. The principal should not be accessed, so the vast majority of a gift is untouchable in all but the direst of circumstances. You have a reserve fund for rainy day purposes and appreciate that it is readily accessible, perfect for emergency needs. On top of those concerns, donors may be reluctant to fund long-term needs instead of offering support to directly benefit mission activities.

You're not wrong. To be sure, there are a number of organizations that function adequately without an endowment. Many of the aforementioned concerns, however, have more to do with timing than anything else. The next chapter will discuss the readiness of an organization for an endowment, the value of a dollar in terms of investment strategy and inflation expectations, and the argument for the best way to navigate the establishment of an endowment.

So why put in the effort for little immediate benefit and a minefield of investment, compliance, and management concerns? As we've discussed, there are two inarguable benefits to the role of the endowment:

- *Motivation.* The ability to contribute to the future of an institution can be a great motivator for many donors. For some, it signifies their enduring dedication to and support of the organization; others may appreciate the opportunity to honor a colleague or loved one with a named fund.
- *Perpetuity and permanence.* An endowment fund is singular in its structure: it supports sustainability and creates an income stream that builds security in operations.

* * * * *

CASE STUDY: THE SLATER MUSEUM
NORWICH, CONNECTICUT

Mission: Located on the campus of the Norwich Free Academy (NFA), the J. F. Slater Memorial Museum awakens visitors to the richness and diversity of the human experience through art and history. For more than one hundred years, the museum has displayed and interpreted the best examples of fine and decorative art, representing a broad range of world cultures of the Americas, Asia, Europe, and Africa.

Founded in 1886 by William Albert Slater, a prominent Connecticut businessman, art collector, and philanthropist, the Slater Museum was established to honor John

Figure 1.2. The Slater Museum. Courtesy of The Slater Museum.

Fox Slater, a philanthropist and Slater's father, known for his advocacy of education of freedmen following the Civil War. The Romanesque Revival building was designed by Massachusetts architect Steven C. Earle and became Earle's best-known commission. Since its establishment, the Slater Museum has been known for its plaster cast collection of Classical and Renaissance era anatomical sculpture, as well as a diverse collection of fine and decorative arts received as gifts from Norwich community residents and alumni of the Norwich Free Academy.

The first of the Slater Museum's five endowments were established in the early twentieth century. The five funds are dedicated to unrestricted operating support, as well as funds restricted for the purposes of programs, acquisitions to the collection, and object conservation. The funds are distributed according to a 5 percent rate determined by a rolling average of the preceding twelve quarters. Since 2007, the funds have been overseen via the separately incorporated NFA Foundation, which oversees the funding of both the academy and the museum, and provides annual financial review of each. This foundation collaborates with the museum leadership to determine fundraising needs and the establishment of new funds, such as the annual fund, which provides support to general operations and funnels support to the unrestricted endowment.

The museum went through a period of transitional leadership in the early 2000s, when the long-serving director retired at the age of eighty-four. Successive leaders of the museum were less experienced with financial oversight, and the relationship with the Academy went through a challenging period. Fueling the fire were concerns that funds restricted for museum use were misappropriated for an Academy capital project. Out of this turmoil emerged a stronger management structure and rigorous audit of the academy finances, the creation of the NFA Foundation, and the appointment of Vivian Zoë as director of the museum.[6] Zoë notes that she has prioritized an allied leadership collaboration with the superintendent of the academy and an adherence to conservative financial management of the museum.

Today, the Slater Memorial Museum functions on an annual budget of $500,000, with approximately 90 percent of that annual budget funded by income distributed from the endowments; the remainder of its expenses—specifically, utilities and maintenance costs—are underwritten by the Norwich Free Academy. As a department of the academy and because of its stable endowment income, the museum has virtually no reliance on earned income, and its only earned revenue stream comes from modest admissions income.

The Slater Memorial Museum maintains a formal relationship with the Norwich Free Academy on whose property it is located, as well as the Norwich Art School, and serves as a resource for the campus and regional communities. While the reliance on academy support is an arrangement that is currently amenable to allow and arguably protects the museum from potentially dynamic market conditions, it precludes the ability to build community relations and independent contributed and earned income support, a common concern for museums that exist as subsidiaries of non-museum entities.

What Can We Learn?

- *Organizations, such as those that function as a department of a larger parent organization, often function as a financial subsidiary.* Understanding of overarching financial activities and policies is necessary to protect the assets of the museum department and to ensure a productive relationship with the parent organization.
- *Institutions face periods of volatility and instability, whether due to a lack of internal controls or because of external circumstances.* Strong leadership and financial structures can help any site weather a storm and potentially emerge more stable than before.

* * * * *

CONCLUSION

In this chapter, the basic definition, structure, and classifications of the endowment were introduced, as well as some of the considerations to keep in mind for how an endowment can benefit an organization in terms of internal structures and external optics. We understand where and when endowments were first established and their evolution to modern usage. Drawbacks and common concerns have been discussed, as well as organization readiness for endowment creation. The endowment provides consistent security and financial support, imperative for sustained operations and to face challenging circumstances. While the time and oversight necessary to build endowments may require patience, a strong endowment can mean the difference between an organization that maintains modest growth over decades versus one that flourishes for three years and is defunct in ten. The next chapter will explore how an organization should prepare itself to establish an endowment and the oversight roles served by staff, trustees, and external advisors.

Key Points: What Have We Learned?

- Endowments are not mandatory according to 501(c)(3) regulations, but a highly effective and sustainable way to ensure regular income and future financial stability.
- Careful cultivation and strategic growth of endowments are necessary for success and as part of future institutional planning.
- There is no organization too small in budget size or too entrenched in a larger parent organization to benefit from an endowment and consistent financial oversight.

NOTES

1. *Stanford University Encyclopedia of Philosophy*, s.v. "Alexander of Aphrodisias," first published October 13, 2003; substantive revision January 19, 2017, https://plato.stanford.edu/entries/alexander-aphrodisias/.
2. Investopedia, "Endowment," by Tim Smith, last updated April 27, 2020, https://www.investopedia.com/terms/e/endowment.asp.
3. Julius Rosenwald, *The Principles of Public Giving* (Washington, DC: Atlantic Monthly, 1929).
4. Ellen Brody, *Charitable Endowments and the Democratization of Dynasty* (Tucson: Arizona Law Review, 1997).
5. Without overly complicating this basic introduction to endowment structures, it is important to note that some funds called "endowments" actually function according to the model forwarded by Julius Rosenwald and are designed to be spent out according to a specified timeframe, defined either when the fund hits a zero balance or according to donor restrictions.
6. Adam Benson, "$70 Million Foundation Keeps NFA Going," *Norwich Bulletin*, January 24, 2015, https://www.norwichbulletin.com/article/20150124/NEWS/150129694.

2

A Head for Business

THE ENDOWMENT AND OPERATIONS

In chapter 1, we introduced the basic elements of the endowment, reviewed terms and definitions, and provided examples of organizations who have established endowments. Let's now turn our attention to exactly *how* an organization prepares to incorporate endowments into its institutional operations and the roles of all involved.

To begin, make sure to do a status check to determine your level of readiness and to understand the financial health of your organization before launching any new initiative that affects its financial infrastructure. Similar to a capital campaign, the creation of a new asset category or subcategory requires proper planning and reflection on the organization, its daily administration, and its leadership. If, for instance, your institution struggles to pay bills and faces deficits every year, this may not be the right time to establish an endowment. Instead, it's probably a good time to attend to your income versus expenses. This chapter will dive into some of the areas of financial health and the particular components of the endowment that comprise strong oversight. As a starting point, you're going to want to reflect upon the following capacities:

- Is the organization currently functioning within its means, or are there consistent issues with meeting expenses?
- Is there confidence at the staff and board levels that the financial systems are being managed most effectively? Is income earned or contributed in anticipation of expenses and according to strong planning practices, or is it a scramble to find contributions to "plug the dam"?
- How strong are your relationships with your donors? Is the organization able to raise funds based on its reputation and established relationships already in place, or does such donor cultivation need to take place?

- How will endowment establishment impact current fundraising activity and the ability to raise support for current needs?
- Does the organization have the staff capacity and board governance in place to competently manage and oversee endowments? How will you collaborate with outside consultation in the form of a fund manager?

Before investing in an endowment strategy, a reflection on the above points is necessary, with particular attention to a strong cash position. This means that an organization should make sure it is regularly meeting its budget needs and has cash or cash equivalents on hand. The cash reserve fund, introduced in chapter 1, is designed to meet short-term or unplanned needs, often referred to as a rainy day fund. A reserve fund serves two major purposes, in that it offers liquidity to the organization. What if you receive a large grant for a capital project, but the funds will not be fully disbursed until after the work is completed and must be paid for? A cash reserve can help meet project costs in the interim (and be replenished after the grant is allocated). What if your boiler dies in the middle of winter? The cash reserve can meet the need without obliterating the budget. The cash reserve fund creates a means by which the organization can access money for immediate needs, and should be established before or concurrent with an endowment, which is best considered a form of long-term support that is *not* readily accessible aside from its regular distribution. Consider forming a reserve fund in the amount of three to six months of operating expenses in cash or in cash equivalents, which are assets with high liquidity like money market funds or mutual funds.

The construction of a cash reserve is a necessary step in building the financial health of organization, in both its function and its optics. Because a cash reserve is typically funded by budget surpluses or other forms of income outside of those necessary to account for annual operating expenses—such as earned revenue that exceeds expectations—it requires a certain degree of activity and an understanding of organizational capacity for its creation. Furthermore, the utility of a cash reserve can be challenging to communicate to less savvy members of your community; some organizations have actually faced pushback from those who question a non-profit organization that solicits public support while sitting on a flush reserve fund.[1] I would recommend looking at this as an opportunity to educate those potential donors about the value of a reserve fund in its unique function to meet emergency needs and to build capacity. And for those donors and potential stakeholders who are a bit savvier, they will recognize that the working capital offered in a strong reserve fund demonstrates stability and the ability to readily handle growth.

The best perspective to have when launching endowment planning is to consider it to be the backbone for institutional stability and a driver for change. The endowment is an investment, both literally and in the cultural evolution of an institution, for its focus on sustainability and long-term planning. And since an endowment will not rectify financial weaknesses or accommodate immediate needs, it is vital to have a functional operational cycle and cash reserve in place before all else.

Another area for review is that of internal and external market conditions. Is this a good time to start an endowment? Think about the economic climate and its impact on philanthropy. The value of the dollar, the stock market, and international trade activity can all impact the viability of investment accounts, including endowments. In times of economic downturn or instability, donors may be less amenable to making large gifts to shore up an endowment that may easily lose money because of market conditions. Trends related to market conditions and to legislation, such as changes in the tax laws, may lead some donors to reduce philanthropic activities. The 2017 Tax Cuts and Jobs Act, for instance, required many donors to consult with their lawyers and financial advisors to understand new regulations regarding charitable giving deductions, and many were advised to suspend their giving until the tax benefits could be better understood. All of these considerations of legal and economic climate do require trustee and staff attention. In the face of economic vulnerability, these considerations may impact institutional readiness to address endowment planning while handling expense management and immediate needs.

The creation of an endowment is a strategic decision, and not one based on meeting short-term needs and goals. In a 2006 article, Mark Hager explains that "endowments are built through the union of an organizational commitment to building an investment reserve and a relationship with donors who believe that this is a good investment in the future, for their community, and for themselves."[2] Organizations must be prepared to commit resources to the conceptualization and the management of a strong endowment program, its oversight policies, and to the relevant relationships with donors. Understanding the endowment structure and function as key to long-term sustainability is essential in communications between board members, staff, and stakeholders.

★ ★ ★ ★ ★

ISSUES IN THE FIELD:
IS THERE EVER A PERFECT TIME TO LAUNCH AN ENDOWMENT?

Let's play devil's advocate for a moment: Is there ever a *perfect* time to establish an endowment? Perhaps you see the allure in a $500,000 unrestricted gift that could be used to shore up a shaky operating year. Why would you invest a gift when you could use it to fund that new exhibition gallery you've always dreamed of? The truth is that the idea of investing a major gift can be difficult to digest, but do not look for excuses not to do so.

This rule can be even more difficult to comprehend during challenging economic times. In dealing with economic downturns, as was the case in 2009 and again in 2020, the conventional wisdom is that funds should be cultivated for immediate needs. And this is certainly true: the 2020 COVID-19 pandemic, for example, forced virtually all museums to close their doors for an extended period of time, which depressed earned income potential and required outreach for additional contributions to offset operating losses. Paramount in times of financial upheaval is the sustenance of the institution. That cannot be overstated. At the same time, data shows that donors are becoming increasingly aware of the value of the endowment.[3] Donors recognize that endowment gifts literally invest in the future of an institution, and endowments are increasingly respected as vital to weathering transition and fluctuations in capacity and activity levels. The endowment provides a worthwhile structure to have in place and with which to navigate planning for and responding to institutional change.

The bottom line is that no organization will ever be successful or stable enough to not welcome gifts for immediate use. That said, it is imperative to rely not on nebulous conceptions of success but on systems of accountability, donor cultivation and gift management, and reporting to determine readiness.

* * * * *

PROPER PROTOCOLS FOR ENDOWMENT MANAGEMENT

Institutional Documentation

This is a good opportunity to review your organization's core documents. This is imperative to do in order to manage endowments properly once an organization is confident in its cash position and financial controls. The next chapter will further explore general institutional planning, but certain guiding resources should be in place.[4] These include the following:

- *Mission statement.* The mission statement is the nucleus of any nonprofit organization and serves to encapsulate the function, purpose, and goals of an organization and guides all operations and leadership actions.
- *Articles of incorporation.* Filed with the state, the articles of incorporation formally document the incorporation, or establishment, of the organization to conduct business.
- *Statement of nonprofit tax exemption.* The nonprofit tax exemption declares that an organization is exempt from, or qualifies for, reduced taxation by state and federal governments. The employer identification number (EIN) is required to seek donations and to do business as a nonprofit incorporation.
- *Bylaws.* The articulation of rules, policies, and procedures of the organization and essential resource for institutional governance.

The mission statement, articles of incorporation, statement of tax exemption, and bylaws are the core documents for legal compliance and organizational direction. Together, these materials allow for the organization to function as a business, to operate exempt from income tax, and to accept donations and other forms of public support. In addition to the above essential documents, the following are also recommended:

- *Vision statement.* Just as the mission statement establishes the work of the nonprofit and its goals, the vision statement addresses the long-term identity of an organization. The impact the institution endeavors to make in its realized state and its position within the context of its community are communicated in a vision statement.
- *Strategic plan.* The strategic plan serves a number of purposes, including the determination of institutional direction and the short-, mid-, and long-term goals necessary to meet these priorities. The plan addresses where and who an institution wishes to be in a certain period of time and details the implementation at operational and governance levels. A strategic plan should be referenced regularly and usually updated at least every five years.
- *Business plan.* If yours is a relatively young organization—and especially if established within the last five years—a business plan is integral in the documentation of business procedures. This document structures the essential functions of the organization and its earned and contributed revenue activities. The business plan is a roadmap for the organization's operations and internal structures and should respond to the strategic plan and vice versa.

The above documents together build a toolbox for legal incorporation, organizational direction, and the current and future identity of an institution. The creation of such resources clarifies an organization's message as well as equips all individuals involved with an understanding of its work.

Personnel Roles and Responsibilities

Endowments are one component of financial management; such financial management is interdependent with sound business practices and compliance. Along with the above written policies, an organization needs to have a confident comprehension of oversight and management roles.

For the smallest organizations, the director will serve to manage the donor cultivation and endowment spending as part of his/her/their management responsibilities. Because of the centralized responsibilities of a small site with only one or two employees, this requires certain precautions be put in place, such as internal controls and division of responsibilities (usually with trustees, such as the treasurer), as well as consistent documentation to ensure stability during future succession planning. Communication between and among departments become increasingly important within larger organizations. The development department is responsible for donor relations, including the cultivation of donors and stewardship reporting, as well as serving as the repository for donor records and gift agreements, including endowment terms. Finance department staff—or a contract bookkeeper—work in tandem with the development team to ensure proper accounting as it relates to the operating budget and expense management. In terms of endowment management, the relationship between the financial and development staff is vital to ensure consistent record-keeping practices are in place. Each endowment fund should be given a project code in the finance department by which fund activity can be easily tracked by all departments. Increasingly, institutions are using integrated software systems, such as Blackbaud or Tessitura, to manage finances, which ensures timely tracking, consistent reporting, and easily accessible data.

Other employees play an important role in endowment management, depending on the terms of the fund. Some endowments may be restricted to support educational programs, in which case the education team will be responsible for ensuring educational programs are compliant with the fund terms; similarly, endowment funds may be utilized to support exhibitions, acquisitions, or conservation activities, in which case the curatorial and collections management staff should report on such activities. Endowments even underwrite staff positions in certain organizations, in which case human resources collaborate with the development department regarding funding. In all of these examples, the development department is the hub of all communications regarding endowment operations, and works with the site director, who oversees the prioritization of activities to be funded, manages relationships with donors, and liaises with trustees and committees of the board regarding endowment spending.

✶ ✶ ✶ ✶ ✶

CASE STUDY: LOS ANGELES COUNTY MUSEUM OF ART
LOS ANGELES, CALIFORNIA

Mission: LACMA's mission is to serve the public through the collection, conservation, exhibition, and interpretation of significant works of art from a broad range of cultures and historical periods, and through the translation of these collections into meaningful educational, aesthetic, intellectual, and cultural experiences for the widest array of audiences.

The Los Angeles County Museum of Art (LACMA) originated as the Los Angeles Museum of History, Science, and Art in 1910, located in Exposition Park, where it remained until 1961. That year, the LACMA was founded as its own institution and with a focus on fine art exhibitions. The LACMA has undergone a series of expansions since its original two buildings opened on Wilshire Boulevard in 1965, which consisted of the Ahmanson Building and the Hammer Building. Subsequent development of the campus included the 1986 construction of the Anderson Building (known as the Art of the Americas Building since 2007), and the Pavilion for Japanese Art in 1988. As a county museum, the LACMA focuses heavily on audience engagement and outreach to Los Angeles County residents. Its focus on

Figure 2.1. Los Angeles County Museum of Art. Photo © Museum Associates / LACMA.

engagement and expansion has proven successful, and the LACMA has doubled its attendance, exhibition program, and campus size since 2007.[5]

Museum Associates, a nonprofit public benefit corporation organized under the laws of the state of California, manages, operates, and maintains the LACMA.[6] Museum Associates consists of fifty-eight trustees and thirteen life trustees that govern the LACMA. The organization functions on an annual budget of approximately $130 million.

The Education and Public Programs department of the LACMA manages all of its educational initiatives. Its annual departmental budget consists of between $1.2 and $1.5 million, and its expenses are met by a combination of contributions, earned revenue from program fees, and unrestricted institutional funds, and endowments restricted to the Education and Public Programs department. Erin Branham, assistant vice president for school and family programs, explained that most institutional funding is allocated to each department from its centrally managed endowment fund, and about 10 percent of the annual department budget is reliant upon this allocation.[7] A variety of endowments have also been established specifically for educational purposes and to underwrite educational initiatives, such as the Bing Fund for Art Education.

The LACMA has maintained a long relationship with the Bing Foundation, dating back to the funding of the 1965 Bing Theatre, a part of the LACMA's original campus. The Bing Foundation has served as a major donor to the LACMA since the

LACMA's earliest years; in the early 2000s, it made a significant donation that included a fund specifically designated for educational purposes. The establishment of the Bing Fund for Art Education was a collaboration between the finance, development, and education departments, with then senior vice president of Education and Family Programs, Jane Burrell, representing the department in the determination of the gift amount and endowment terms, which simply state that the Bing Fund is intended to "provide art education for children."[8]

Today, the extremely open terms of the Bing Fund for Art Education make it, according to Branham, the "perfect endowment." Because of its flexibility, the use of the Bing Fund has evolved since its establishment in 2005. Since it is restricted for education purposes, the Fund is managed at the discretion of the Education and Public Programs Department. Annual reporting is provided to the Bing Foundation, a collaboration with finance and development departments of the museum, and provides an overview of the programs supported by the fund and its ongoing impact. Branham offers that the fund is a terrific resource for its reliability and its alleviation of pressure on revenue generation.

What Can We Learn?

- *Endowments restricted for specific departments can be extremely beneficial in supporting basic functions of the organization.* The more open the terms of the fund, the greater its utility and relevance as the organization grows its work.
- *Communication between departments is key.* When a funder expresses interest in a particular service area, incorporate a relevant team member into the cultivation of the donor, the establishment of the terms, and the annual reporting process.

* * * * *

Consistent and participatory trustee governance is absolutely vital to strong endowment oversight. Along with the daily administration of endowment funds at the staff level, the board is charged with all fiduciary oversight of the organization, including endowments. Like other functions of a board, the endowment oversight takes place via an investment committee, which consists of board members (and others, if the institutional bylaws allow) who review fund balances in the context of the market and liaise with investment advisors. Staff members, such as the director and representatives of the finance department, may also sit on the committee in an ex officio and informational capacity. The investment committee and its functions should be outlined in a committee charter and should align with the institutional bylaws.

The investment committee responsibilities can include oversight of investment advisors, the determination of investment goals and priorities, and working in conjunction with other committees of the board. The audit committee oversees the completion of the annual audit, which often incorporates the review of the investment and spending policy as well as the fund balances incorporated in the documentation of institutional assets. Likewise, the finance committee benefits from regular communication with the investment committee as they review the financial health and needs of an organization and the endowment distribution expectations. And of course, the treasurer of the board functions in collaboration with all three committees and in representation of the board regarding financial matters.

While neither involved in the daily management of the fund, which the staff executes, nor the regular oversight of endowment and other institutional funds, which is handled at the investment committee level, the board is responsible for institutional direction and fiduciary concerns. The investment committee should regularly report the status of investments to the board at its meetings, separate from staff and treasurer reporting. In its approval of the annual budget, the board should consider the endowment distribution and its documentation in the budget composition. The board also votes on all institutional policies, including the investment policy, and any changes to the endowment spending rule. Don't forget that the board can designate any unrestricted funds for a particular use, known as a board-designated fund (see chapter 1).

The roles of the staff and board members may make perfect sense, but you may be intimidated by the actual oversight of the endowments. Who is responsible for actually investing the funds and for understanding the market? Rely on the experts for this work. Regardless of the expertise offered by the members of the investment committee, direct fund management by a volunteer investment committee is increasingly rare, and it is prudent to hire an external financial advisor to oversee investment activities. Registered investment advisors (RIAs) are licensed to invest funds, and many specialize in endowments and work with a variety of account sizes (none too small!). RIAs handle investing of funds on behalf of the organization, and often in consultation with the financial staff and the investment committee. Along with other contracted services and partner institutions—such as the bank that maintains your cash accounts, and any contracted accounting services for bookkeeping or auditing purposes—external expertise is not only welcome but necessary for compliance purposes.

THE INVESTMENT COMMITTEE CHARTER AND THE INVESTMENT POLICY

Like all committees of a board, the investment committee must document its activities and its role in a charter. The committee charter is different from the investment policy in that the charter outlines responsibilities, procedures, and general activities of the committee, while the policy articulates the investment objectives of the committee (see figure 2.2).

The investment policy is the seminal document in the oversight of all investment activities of an organization, whether incorporated as a nonprofit or a for-profit entity. For-profit corporations formalize their investment business via an

BOARD OF REGENTS
SMITHSONIAN INSTITUTION

CHARTER OF THE INVESTMENT COMMITTEE

JANUARY 2022

I. **Establishment by the Board of Regents**

The Bylaws of the Board of Regents establish the Investment Committee. *See* Bylaw 4.07.

II. **Statement of Purpose**

The purpose of the Investment Committee is to assist the Board of Regents (1) providing oversight of the Institution's endowment, strategy, and investment guidelines and (2) performing such related functions as may be assigned to it by the Board of Regents. *See* Bylaw 4.07.

III. **Appointment Membership, and Length of Service**

A. Appointment

1. The Investment Committee shall consist of no fewer than two (2) and no more than six (6) Regent members. The Committee may also consist of non-Regent members well-chosen for their expertise of relevance to the duties and responsibilities of the Committee.

2. With approval of the Board of Regents, the members of the Investment Committee shall be appointed by the Chancellor.

3. The Board of Regents, in accepting the Report of the Nominating Committee (now Governance and Nominating Committee) on January 6, 2003, provided that:

a) Sitting committee chairs may recommend to the Governance and Nominating Committee the preferred membership and chairmanship for their respective committees for the ensuing calendar year.

b) The Governance and Nominating Committee proposes for the Regents' consideration at the first Regents' meeting of each calendar year a motion including recommended memberships and chairmanships for all committees.

Figure 2.2. Smithsonian Institution investment subcommittee charter. Courtesy of the Smithsonian Institution.

B. Membership

    1. All members of the Investment Committee shall be free of any conflict of interest with respect to the matters before the Committee.

    2. In light of the special expertise required to execute the duties of the Investment Committee, the composition of the Committee may consist of a majority of non-Regent members as long as at least two members are Regents.

    3. All members shall be subject to the Investment Committee's Ethics Guidelines. In addition, non-Regent members shall be subject to the same ethics guidelines as apply to the Regents.

C. Length of Service

    1. With the approval of the Board of Regents, a Regent may serve on the Investment Committee for the length of his or her term as a Regent, but in no event longer than twelve (12) years. With the approval of the Board of Regents, a non-Regent may serve up to eight (8) years as a non-Regent member of the Investment Committee.

    2. The Board of Regents, in accepting the Report of the Nominating Committee on January 6, 2003, provided that a Regent may be appointed as a Regent Emeritus and encouraged to continue his or her service to the Smithsonian by serving as many as but no more than three (3) years on selected committees following his or her active service as a Regent. The Governance and Nominating Committee and the Investment Committee Chair will review the effectiveness of any Investment Committee member in its annual nominations.

IV. Rules for the Conduct of Meetings of the Investment Committee

A. Investment Committee Policies and Procedures

The Investment Committee shall have the power to adopt rules for the conduct of its business with respect to all matters not provided for in the Bylaws of, or as provided by, the Board of Regents. *See* Bylaw 4.11.

B. Chair

    1. The Committee Chair shall be appointed by the Chancellor and the Board of Regents. [*See* Bylaw 4.11]. Both Regents and non-Regents are eligible to be Chair of the Investment Committee.

2. If the Chair is unable to attend a meeting, the members will be polled prior to that meeting and a substitute Chair, for the purposes of that meeting only, will be identified among those members who have indicated that they will be present.

C. Meetings

1. The Investment Committee will hold not less than three (3) meetings each year and such additional meetings as the Investment Committee Chair may deem necessary or appropriate.

2. The Committee Chair or any three members of the Investment Committee may call special meetings of the Committee.

3. Notice of the meetings of the Investment Committee may be given by hand delivery, by deposit in the U.S. Mail, by express mail, by electronic facsimile, or by electronic mail.

4. Members of the Investment Committee will be provided an agenda in advance of each meeting.

5. The meetings of the Investment Committee may be conducted in person, by video conference, or by telephone conference call.

6. If a majority of the Investment Committee agrees, the Committee may conduct business via facsimile or electronic format without a meeting. The vote of a majority of the Committee by facsimile, electronic format, or other method as approved by the Committee Chair, shall constitute the action of the Committee.

D. Quorum

1. Section 4.10 of the Bylaws of the Board of Regents provides:

. . . [A] majority of the members of all standing and special committees as may be established by the Board shall constitute a quorum.

2. In the absence of a quorum, a lesser number may adjourn the meeting.

V.   Responsibilities and Duties of the Investment Committee

A. The responsibilities and duties of the Investment Committee shall include the following:

Figure 2.2. (*Continued*)

1. Review the Institution's investment policy and strategies and provide policy guidance to management and, as directed, to the Board of Regents. Such guidance shall include but not be limited to:

   a) Overall investment strategy and guidelines for the endowment,

   b) Evaluation of asset classes for investment,

   c) Selection of new investment managers,

   d) Termination of existing investment managers, and

   e) Review of the performance of the endowment fund and its investment managers.

VI.   Communications and Minutes

A. The Committee Chair will report orally or in writing to the Board of Regents on other matters discussed at the most recent Committee meeting.

B. Minutes of each meeting of the Investment Committee will be prepared. Draft minutes will be provided to all members for their review and, upon approval, will be made a part of the official record of the proceedings of the Board of Regents. If the Committee has not approved the minutes prior to the next full Regents' meeting, draft minutes will be provided to the Board. The Board will be informed subsequent to their meeting if any significant changes are made in the final version of the Investment Committee minutes. The official record of the Board of Regents' proceedings for any given Regents' meeting will incorporate the latest version of the Investment Committee's minutes at the time the official record is published.

VII.   Resources and Authority

A. Staff Support and the Retention of Outside Advisors and Consultants

The Committee may, without further action by the Board of Regents, retain any external advisors, attorneys, consultants, and accountants (collectively "Advisors") it deems necessary to carry out the Committee's responsibilities. The Smithsonian will adequately fund the costs and expenses of these Advisors under arrangements that assure the independence of these Advisors and their loyalty to the Institution, the Board of Regents, and the Committee. *See* Bylaw 4.09.

B. Indemnification

Section 2.12 of the Bylaws of the Board of Regents provides:

...Members of the Committee may be indemnified for any and all liabilities and reasonable expenses incurred in connection with any claim, action, suit, or proceeding arising from present or past service for the Smithsonian Institution, in accordance with resolutions adopted by the Board.

C. Expenses

1. Section 4.11 of the Bylaws of the Board of Regents provides:

   . . . Expenses of members in attending meetings of committees established by the Board of Regents, including travel expenses to and from the place of meeting, may be paid by the Institution . . . .

2. It is understood that expenses claimed shall be appropriate and reasonable, in keeping with the Smithsonian's nature as a public trust.

VIII. Periodic Review

A. Charter Review

1. As part of its duties to assist the Board of Regents in providing oversight of the Institution's endowment, overall investment strategy, and guidelines for the endowment, the Committee may propose changes to this Charter.

2. The Committee will review and assess at least annually the adequacy of the Investment Committee Charter. In consultation with the Governance and Nominating Committee, the Committee will submit proposed revisions to the Board of Regents for its approval.

B. Committee Performance

The Committee will at least annually evaluate its own performance with respect to the requirements of the Charter in such a manner as the Committee, in consultation with the Governance and Nominating Committee, deems appropriate.

Figure 2.2. (*Continued*)

investment policy, including employee pension and retirement accounts, and are referenced in corporation documents and in annual reports. In nonprofit corporations, the investment policy documents investment activities, including but not limited to accountable parties, cash thresholds, and distribution rules and procedures, among other topics.

An investment policy is an essential resource to guide financial activities of an organization, relevant to daily operations and regular endowment oversight as well as institutional direction and compliance, such as the annual audit process, in which endowments are documented as an asset category. A successful investment policy is articulate, specific, and is regularly reviewed by the investment committee and the full board to ensure that it is current and properly documents the organization's activities related to investments. An investment policy protects the organization from imprudent spending, guides activities during transitions in senior staffing and board oversight, and informs financial advisors.

When establishing an investment policy, there are certain elements you will wish to include. Consider the following topics and questions as you build your investment policy:

- *Definition of investment strategy and goals.* What is the purpose of your investment activity? Does your organization wish to sustain its current level, to grow specific funds to support particular activities? Or does it wish to grow the distribution amount and its function in the annual operating budget? Make sure that your investment committee, and board as a whole, understands the function and goals of the investments and their income.
- *Delegation of accountability.* Define the duties and responsibilities of all involved including staff, the investment committee, and the role of trustees. Though it is not necessary to be overly specific about the work of an external RIA since those arrangements should be addressed in a separate service contract, it is a good idea to reference and include the contract as a supplemental binding legal agreement.
- *Diversification guidelines.* What is your ideal asset allocation, and according to what breakdown will funds be invested? Your investment portfolio will consist of a mix of stocks, fixed income, and commodities. You will also have the option to invest domestically or internationally, by company size or industry. Diversification allows for a mixture of assets; this is important because different asset classes react differently to the same economic event.[9] These discussions are typically held at the investment committee level in consultation with the RIA. Such conversations may also include environmental, social, and governance priorities (see chapter 5).
- *Monitoring criteria.* Will you have performance and market thresholds in place to determine redistribution of funds? There is no crystal ball for the economy, and it is likely that certain investments will not perform as expected, either due to fluctuations in the economy as a whole or in specific industries. If a

trade deal falls through, for example, an investment in a company reliant on international distribution could perform poorly and lose value. Consider a data point, such as a percentage of starting value, at which a fund may be due for reinvestment.

- *Threshold terms.* Will you have criteria to determine how to "name" an endowment? Consider if there will be a financial threshold instituted that must be met in order for a donor to earn a named endowment, similar to naming opportunities in capital projects, or if the organization will allow any endowment to be named without a threshold. Another determination will be at what point a fund *becomes* an endowment: At what value will an endowment be considered a true endowment versus a pre-endowment fund? Many organizations institute a dollar amount threshold that must be met before any fund can be considered an endowment and annually distribute income. A pre-endowment is typically left to grow in value, though it can be accessed with the donor's approval. Consider if a threshold policy will be reasonable for your organization and if so, scaled to organizational size, budget, and use.

THE INVESTMENT POLICY: THE DISTRIBUTION RATE

A topic of critical importance in the investment policy is the establishment of the annual distribution rate. The distribution rate is the calculation by which the annual amount of the distribution for use is determined. Perhaps the most relevant definition is provided by the National Association of College and University Business Officers (NACUBO), and states that the distribution rate

> represents the distribution for spending divided by the beginning market value (endowment value on or around the beginning of the fiscal year). The distribution for spending is the dollar amount withdrawn from the endowments to support expenditures as determined and defined by each institution. The rate is calculated net of investment fees and expenses for managing the endowment.[10]

The distribution rate is, to be clear, not a synonym for interest earnings, which is a common mistake. Instead, it is a calculation based on the total return of the fund, which is the full return on an investment, inclusive of interest and also income generated from dividend or rental payments and changes in the fund's market value. Because the distribution rate determines exactly how much of the invested funds will be used to underwrite expenses in each year, it is an important decision that requires thorough review by the investment committee and full board approval before any revisions take place.

The common rule of thumb is the "4 percent rule," which is considered the amount of income that can be spent from an investment year to year while maintaining the principal. This rule applies to for-profit and nonprofit entities, and even extends to how many individuals manage retirement and pension funds. According to the American Alliance of Museums, the best practice for American museums is a distribution rate between 4 and 5 percent of the endowment value.[11] Why 4 percent? This figure is commonly used because it allows for a fund to grow in value in consideration of inflation rates and preserving the principle.

So, is it really that simple? Do all organizations just calculate 4 percent of the market value of a fund at the beginning of the year and call it a day? Well, that's one option, but there are a few ways to calculate the distribution rate. The 4 percent rule is an excellent and consistent guideline, though many organizations shift their distribution slightly each year. This chart by NACUBO (shown in figure 2.3) illustrates these variances:

Average Annual Effective Spending Rates* for U.S. College and University Endowments and Affiliated Foundations, Fiscal Years 2018 to 2009

Size of Endowment	2018 %	2017 %	2016 %	2015 %	2014 %	2013 %	2012 %	2011 %	2010 %	2009 %
Over $1 Billion	4.6	4.8	4.4	4.3	4.6	4.8	4.7	5.2	5.6	4.6
$501 Million to $1 Billion	4.2	4.6	4.3	4.1	4.3	4.6	4.7	5.2	5.7	4.9
$251 Million to $500 Million	4.4	4.4	N/A	N/A	N/A	N/A	N/A	N/A	N/A	N/A
$101 Million to $250 Million	4.4	4.6	4.3	4.1	4.3	4.4	4.3	5.0	4.9	4.4
$51 Million to $100 Million	4.6	4.5	4.4	4.4	4.4	4.4	4.3	4.5	4.6	4.7
$25 Million to $50 Million	4.1	4.2	4.1	4.0	4.2	4.3	3.8	4.0	4.1	4.3
Under $25 Million	4.1	4.0	3.8	4.5	4.6	4.1	3.7	3.7	3.5	3.9
Type of Institution										
All Public Institutions	3.8	4.1	4.0	4.0	4.1	4.1	4.0	4.5	4.1	4.2
Public College, University or System	3.8	4.1	4.0	3.8	3.8	4.2	3.9	4.3	4.3	3.7
Institution-Related Foundations	3.8	4.1	3.9	4.2	4.3	4.0	4.0	4.1	3.9	4.3
Combined Endowment/Foundation	3.9	4.2	4.1	3.9	4.2	4.4	4.2	5.9	4.6	4.5
All Private Colleges and Universities	4.7	4.6	4.4	4.3	4.5	4.6	4.3	4.6	4.8	4.5
Average (All Institutions)	4.4	4.4	4.3	4.2	4.4	4.4	4.2	4.6	4.5	4.4

All data are for years ending June 30. Data for 2009 through 2017 are from the NACUBO-Commonfund Study of Endowments.

*The effective spending rate represents the distribution for spending divided by the beginning market value (endowment value on or around the beginning of the fiscal year). The distribution for spending is the dollar amount withdrawn from the endowments to support expenditures on student financial aid, faculty research, maintenance of facilities, and other campus operations, as determined and defined by each institution. The rate is calculated net of investment fees and expenses for managing the endowment.

Data for fiscal year 2008 come from the 2008 NACUBO Endowment Study. N/A means not available.

Figure 2.3. This table illustrates the typical spend rate for colleges and universities between 2009 and 2018. Courtesy of the National Association of College and University Business Officers.

In the goal to strategize short-term funding needs and its relationship to fund values, many organizations take different approaches to determining their distribution rate. The methods commonly utilized tend to follow one of three types of distribution rates:

- *Simple (or fixed) distribution.* Focused on conserving the principal or corpus of a fund, the simple distribution rate is the strictest and determined solely by the fund value at the beginning of the year. While this approach does the job of conserving the principal, it does not allow for any responsiveness to market conditions or to institutional needs. Because it follows such a strict calculation, funding can be highly volatile from year to year and hard to incorporate into budget planning because of its high sensitivity to the market.
- *Inflation-based distribution.* The rate is determined by applying the current inflation rate to last year's spending. This model is the polar opposite of the simple distribution calculation: it is highly predictable and has virtually no reaction to market conditions. It still creates challenges, however, in that it is wholly internally focused and based on year-to-year spending of the institution and easily skewed by inconsistencies in spending.
- *Smoothed (or hybrid) distribution.* The distribution is calculated as a rolling average of the fund value over a period of time. As you may expect, this is the Goldilocks of the distribution calculation models. The most common approach to distribution rate determination, the smoothed approach allows for some variability, but not too much. The longer the moving average (typically between twelve and twenty-four quarters), the greater the smoothing effect.[12]

The investment policy serves to formalize internal processes, investment committee and board oversight responsibilities, and consistency in donor relations. The policy also serves an external purpose, affirming to potential donors, stakeholders, and even auditors that the organization is committed to consistent and transparent

Figure 2.4. Natural History Museum of Utah. Courtesy of the Natural History Museum of Utah.

funds oversight and sustainability. Many organizations, such as the Smithsonian Institution, now share their investment policies publicly, a signal to the general public of compliant and sound business practices.

* * * * *

CASE STUDY: NATURAL HISTORY MUSEUM OF UTAH
SALT LAKE CITY, UTAH

Mission: The museum's mission is to illuminate the natural world and the place of humans within it, and we do this in the context of the extraordinary landscape of Utah. We are a part of and draw on the unique intellectual resources of the University of Utah.

The Natural History Museum of Utah was founded in 1967 and originally housed in the George Thomas Building at the University of Utah. The Utah State Legislature established the museum and assigned it to the University of Utah before its construction; because of its affiliation with the state, the museum does not hold a memorandum of understanding with the University of Utah, though the university owns its property and building. The Natural History Museum is responsible for the stewardship of vertebrae fossils and archeological findings. Today, the museum's collections number more than 1.6 million objects, many of which have been acquired via donation, purchase, or transferal from university academic departments.

In 2011, the Natural History Museum relocated to a new building on campus, the Rio Tinto Center, which includes spaces for gallery, program, and research functions. The project cost more than $100 million and was supported by the university, federal and state agencies, and direct fundraising initiatives. The museum maintains its own twenty-three-member board of advisors, designed to provide consultation and support on key issues facing the museum. The museum is currently in the midst of a five-year strategic plan that includes financial sustainability; endowment growth is cited as a goal of the institution.[13] The museum functions on an annual budget of approximately $12 million, which does not include those costs underwritten by the University of Utah, including certain administrative functions, utilities, facilities, and insurance expenses.

According to Sarah George, former executive director of the Natural History Museum and current chief philanthropy officer–campus—a role in which she oversees all campus planned giving, annual giving, and advancement policies and procedures—the amount of the endowment distribution allocated to the museum is typically quite small and accounts from roughly 1 percent of the total budget.[14] A small number of funds that are restricted for museum activities support scholarships, programs, operations, and collections management. The remainder of the 1 percent allocation is unrestricted.

As is typical with university endowment management, the individual endowments are invested en masse and as one large pool managed centrally by the university. The distribution is calculated quarterly according to the 4 percent rate, and the allocation to the museum transferred by the Investment Management Office to the museum via an expendable account for museum use. The university entertains a system in which allocations that are left unspent in part or in full, as well as additional funds such as operating surpluses, can be reinvested as contributions to a central pool. George took advantage of this system while she was executive director, shifting a portion of the operating surplus to the fund instead of transferring the surplus to the reserve fund. After a year, the pooled fund generates 4 percent for distribution, in keeping with the endowment rate followed by the university; after five years, the university allows access to the full value of the fund in addition to its annual distribution. Essentially, the fund functions as a quasi endowment, and George's strategy of transferring two-thirds of the museum's budget surplus to its reserve and one-third to the pooled fund has paid off handsomely: by the end of George's tenure as director in 2019, the Natural History Museum had grown its $30,000 annual contribution to the pool to a value of $750,000 while maintaining a cash reserve of $2 million. This leaves the museum in an extremely healthy financial position as its new executive director, Jason Cryan, takes the helm.

What Can We Learn?

- *The annual endowment distribution is for many organizations a vital component of their funding plan.* But what if you don't need it all? A wise idea is to conserve and grow unspent distribution and surplus funds via reinvestment.
- *Prioritize a healthy cash reserve before undertaking long-term investments.* The Natural History Museum had reached a strong cash position before creating its quasi-endowment system, but continues to support its reserve from its annual operating surplus.

* * * * *

CONCLUSION

As noted in this chapter, strong and articulate policy and communications systems are vital for a resilient and relevant endowment program. We considered the roles of the board and the staff regarding preparedness and consideration of the internal and external climate and readiness for the introduction of an endowment program. Additionally, this chapter introduced the components of a comprehensive endowment management policy for reference. These will serve an important foundation for the discussions of endowments and institutional planning in the next chapter.

Key Points: What Have We Learned?

- Make sure your organization is well-positioned to solicit and accept gifts to an endowment fund. The establishment of strong oversight and administration protocols create the framework for consistent, transparent, and stable endowment management.
- Endowments are a long game and not for immediate payoff. As tempting as it may be to accept major gifts for immediate use, and while there is certainly a time and a place for such gifts, endowments are an essential component of a financially sustainable development program.

NOTES

1. Scott E. Stewart, "Five Steps to Starting an Endowment: Even Smaller Nonprofits Can," *Candid* (blog), March 2, 2020, https://blog.candid.org/post/five-steps-to -starting-an-endowment-even-smaller-nonprofits-can/.
2. Mark Hager, "Should Your Organization Build an Endowment?" *Nonprofit Quarterly*, December 10, 2019, https://nonprofitquarterly.org/should-your-nonprofit-build-an -endowment/.
3. Indiana University—Purdue University Indianapolis Lilly Family School of Philanthropy, *Giving USA 2020: The Annual Report on Philanthropy for the Year 2019* (Indianapolis: Lilly Family School of Philanthropy, June 16, 2020), https://philanthropy .iupui.edu/news-events/news-item/giving-usa-2020:-charitable-giving-showed -solid-growth,-climbing-to-$449.64-billion-in-2019,-one-of-the-highest-years-for -giving-on-record.html?id=328.
4. For more information regarding the establishment of core documents, see Rebekah Beaulieu, *Financial Fundamentals for Historic House Museums* (Lanham, MD: Rowman & Littlefield, 2017).
5. "History," Los Angeles County Museum of Art, accessed August 1, 2021, https:// www.lacma.org/about?tab=history#history.
6. Los Angeles County Museum of Art 990 Return of Organization Exempt from Tax, 2018, available at https://pdf.guidestar.org/PDF_Images/2018/952/264/ 2018-952264067-10cb3358-9.pdf?_ga=2.115506318.983356654.1606224121 -14764229.1604591678.
7. Erin Branham, interview with Rebekah Beaulieu, November 23, 2020.
8. Erin Branham, interview with Rebekah Beaulieu, November 23, 2020.
9. Kimberly Amadeo, "Diversified Investment Examples," *The Balance*, July 24, 2020, https://www.thebalance.com/what-is-a-diversified-investment-3305834#:~ :text=Updated%20July%2004%2C%202020,to%20the%20same%20eco nomic%20event.
10. National Association of College and University Business Officers, "2018 Nacu-bo-TIAA Study of Endowments," *National Association of College and University Business Officers*, January 31, 2019. https://www.nacubo.org/Press-Releases/2019/ US-Educational-Endowments-Report-8-2-Percent-Return-in-FY18.

11. Elizabeth Merritt, "The Future of Funding—Revisited," *Center for the Future of Museums* (blog), May 5, 2015, https://www.aam-us.org/2015/05/05/the-future-of-funding-revisited/.

12. "Endowment Spending Policies," *Buckingham Strategic Wealth*, September 3, 2021, https://buckinghamstrategicwealth.com/uploads/archive/March-2019.pdf.

13. "Mission and Goals," Natural History Museum of Utah, accessed August 1, 2021, https://nhmu.utah.edu/museum/about/mission-values.

14. Sarah George, interview with the Rebekah Beaulieu, November 23, 2020.

3

A Strong Backbone

INSTITUTIONAL PLANNING AND ENDOWMENTS

As noted in chapters 1 and 2, a strong understanding of the structures of endowments is vital to healthy endowment management. We have reviewed the terminology and systems common in endowment functions, as well as the role of a board of directors and their mandate of fiduciary oversight of all institutional assets, including endowments. A board is charged with the establishment and revision of institutional policies and in the context of endowments, and it is important to recognize that includes guidance regarding use and spending levels.

While a board is responsible for the governance of the funds as a component of institutional and fiduciary health, the regular management of endowment funds is the responsibility of the staff. In very large organizations, there may be staff positions dedicated solely to endowment management and investments. In most museums, advisement is outsourced to licensed financial firms or community foundations, with internal accounts management divided between development and business offices. The fundraising team is responsible for donor relations, inclusive of the establishment of the funds, use and distribution terms, as well as regular stewardship and donor reporting. The financial staff, on the other hand, manages the documentation of the financial performance of each fund, usually generated by the outside advisors, the tracking of spending from endowments and in keeping with donor intent, and liaises with the investment and/or finance committees, board of trustees, and treasurer regarding spending. This chapter focuses on the internal financial management of endowments for operational purposes, special projects, and planning activities.

Once the endowments have been established, any internal and/or donor-advised use thresholds have been reached, and the distribution is active, endowments should be a fundamental component of the resource base of the institution. For some organizations, endowment use is for special purposes, as will be illustrated in this chapter's case studies; for others, it is essential to operations. Let's begin with a discussion of how endowment income used to underwrite operating activity is administered.

ENDOWMENTS USED TO FUND REGULAR OPERATIONS

For many organizations, the income from endowment distribution is incorporated into the sources of funding available to offset operating costs, along with contributed income, which consists of grants and sponsorships, individual donations, and government support at municipal, state, and federal levels; and earned income, which is received in exchange for goods and services, such as admissions, program fees, and merchandise sales. Endowments are typically tracked as part of institutional income, which is the income that is generated internally and may include annual endowment distributions and available spend-down funds, for which no corpus is preserved and often used for current projects or purposes. Institutional income can generate typically 30 percent of an organization's operating sources. Some nonprofits might be more reliant on such income, while others are less so.

For those organizations that utilize an endowment to underwrite operating costs, the annual operating budget structure is dependent on the amount of funds available and as calculated annually in accordance with the spending policy. This calculation is determined every year, along with and dependent on the market valuation of the endowment fund. Such information also informs the annual financial statements and audit review, which includes a disclosure of the spending policy and market valuation in the statement of financial position. As the annual operating budget is approved by the board of trustees under their mandate of fiduciary oversight, this approval is an opportunity to assess the utility of the distribution in relation to budget needs, and can serve as a refresher for those trustees who do not serve on the financial or investment committees. Museums that are subsidiaries or departments of larger organizations, such as national membership organizations like the Daughters of the American Revolution or the Colonial Dames of America, as well as those funded as part of academic institutions or municipalities, may benefit from endowment funding, but without direct management of their resources themselves. Such situations may mean that the allocation of operating support is determined by the parent organization and may not allow for planning at individual sites. In these cases, the benefit of additional communication throughout a reporting period is that much more important, and not simply at the start or end of a budget cycle.

Organizations that are self-governing have the opportunity to establish strong reporting and review protocols throughout the year, which can serve to guide investment activities at the board level and to direct planning activities for the staff. On a quarterly basis, the investment committee reviews fund performance reports, as noted in chapter 2; based on these reports, committee members may elect to reinvest funds based on market conditions, economic trends, and past performance of the investments. At the staff level, this quarterly system can also create a structured schedule for the quarterly review of spending in the context of the operating budget and special projects.

DISCRETIONARY FUND MANAGEMENT

One central unrestricted endowment fund can be relatively straightforward to manage, but what if you have a number of restricted funds? Funds with restriction terms may not be available for operational use, but instead to be used only when there exists an expense that conforms with the use terms of the original endowment gift and as stated in the gift acceptance documentation. Museums that are well established may have endowment funds with particular use restrictions dating one hundred years ago that could be a challenge to track. For that reason, I recommend a template such as this one (shown in figure 3.1) to track spending, use restrictions, and annual market values of the funds.

As you can see, a template such as the one shown in figure 3.1 can be an easy and accessible reference for both fundraising and financial team members to record relevant information. Columns for project codes allow for easy tracking in your accounting software, and a column to note which funds are available to underwrite operating expenses as opposed to those to be used according to strict terms are also included. Figure 3.2 shows an example of a template populated with information.

Figure 3.2 includes information for funds restricted to acquisitions, conservation and collections care, salaries, and program funds. Because salaries are an operating expense, they are designated to support operating needs, and they would be included as an institutional income source in the annual operating budget. Other funds, such as the acquisition funds, do not support general operating activities, but are available for specific, relevant purchases. The Rita Hayworth Fund goes one step further and specifies the type of acquisition it can be used for, which limits its funding to Mexican art and objects. Some funds, like the Buddy Holly and Little Richard funds, are housed in the program funds category, but could be used for other purposes. The Buddy Holly Fund can be used for exhibitions but is available for museum support—hence its inclusion as a fund to underwrite operations—and the Little Richard Fund could be used for acquisitions if needed.

Comprehensive understanding of endowments is not limited to fund balances and spending policies. With a clear understanding of donor intent and use restrictions, we can actively and dynamically manage endowments to benefit general operations and accommodate special needs. When paired with consistent transaction spending, such as in the completion of monthly reconciliations of transactions, the endowments can be an integral component of the planning process. Just like all financial processes, organizations benefit most from consistent and active management of their endowment funds, which in turn supports strategic project planning, special initiatives, and effective spending.

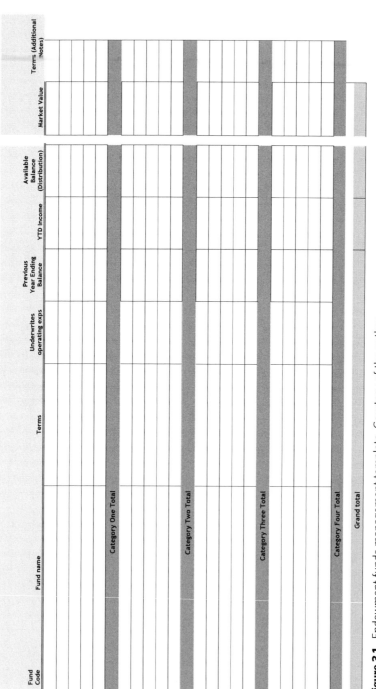

Figure 3.1. Endowment funds management template. Courtesy of the author.

Fund Code	Fund name	Terms	Underwrites operating exps	Previous Year Ending Balance	YTD Income	Available Balance (Distribution)	Market Value	Terms (Additional Notes)
100001	Marilyn Monroe Collection Purchase Fund	unrestricted acquisn		316.80	1,088.53	1,405.33	2,987.00	for the purchase of Art Objects
100002	Elizabeth Taylor Fund	unrestricted acquisn		1,614.83	2,758.78	4,373.61	7,424.00	for the purchase of Art Objects
100003	Rita Hayworth Acquisition Fund	restricted acquisn - Mexican Art		15,141.86	15,685.32	5,778.94	41,639.00	acquisition: Mexican art and heritage focus
	Acquisitions Funds Total			17,073.49	19,532.63	11,557.88	52,050.00	
100011	Marlon Brando Fund for Collections Stewardship	unrestricted conservation needs		3,502.30	1,525.00	5,027.30	39,560.00	in support of collections needs, equipment
100012	Paul Newman Art Conservation Fund	restricted conservation - permanent collection only		6,524.11	2,016.28	7,940.39	54,910.00	for the conservation of works of art
	Conservation/Collections Care Funds Total			10,026.41	3,541.28	12,967.69	94,470.00	
100021	Patsy Cline Foundation Grant	support curator	x	5,725.00	2,300.00	8,025.00	68,125.00	to support curator of salary
100022	Ella Fitzgerald Museum of Art Directorship Fund	support director	x	-	3,618.82	3,618.82	37,050.00	to support director salary
	Salaries Funds Total			5,725.00	5,918.82	11,643.82	105,175.00	
100030	Buddy Holly Museum of Art Fund	unrestricted - general exhibitions	x	-	6,906.00	6,906.00	43,025.00	in support of Museum of Art
100031	Elvis Presley Excellence Fund	restricted to music education		4,349.17	3,102.25	7,451.42	53,421.00	for guitar classes
100032	Little Richard Endowment Fund	cd be used for acquis'n		7,694.88	6,308.31	14,003.19	97,858.00	programs or acquisitions
	Program Funds Total			12,044.05	16,316.56	28,360.61	194,304.00	
	Grand total			44,868.95	45,309.29	90,178.24	445,999.00	

Figure 3.2. Endowment funds management sample. Courtesy of the author.

ENDOWMENTS USED TO FUND SPECIAL PROJECTS

As we see from our sample templates, many endowment funds are accompanied by restrictions that prohibit their use for general operations. While we *always* want to encourage as few restrictions as possible, there are certainly ways to make restricted funds work to your advantage. Consider where there may be potential flexibilities, such as in our Buddy Holly and Little Richard funds: Are you looking to invest in a major acquisition? Perhaps you do not have funds comfortably available in your acquisitions fund, and you're looking for an alternative. Since the restriction of the Little Richard Fund allows for use to support acquisitions, you would be fully compliant in redirecting those funds from programs to acquisitions. Discretionary endowment management allows organizations to utilize endowments in accordance with use restrictions, and to plan for project needs or adapt in times of unforeseen crisis or institutional evolution.

When some organizations realize a budget surplus, they shore up their reserve funds, which is immediately accessible if needed, or invest the surplus to grow their endowment, both of which are prudent financial measures. In our discretionary oversight of restricted funds, we can also see the benefit of exercising conservative management. If you do not need to use the distribution from a restricted fund in a given year, it is a great idea to let the distribution balance grow. This allows you to develop the amount distributed from the fund without disrupting the corpus. It can be done in anticipation of budget scale and funding needs. Perhaps you wish to host modestly scaled exhibitions for one year, in order to fund a major exhibition in the next year. Or your curatorial team and collections committee agree to allow the acquisitions funds to be used sparingly for two years, which allows for distributed funds to be available for more expensive potential acquisitions in the third year. As long as the fund use aligns with the donor restrictions, discretionary fund management can be a keen way to approach operating *and* special needs.

ENDOWMENTS AND INSTITUTIONAL PLANNING

The management of endowment spending is a component of the administration of operating activities, and restricted funds support specific needs. Another consideration is how endowments relate to institutional planning. We see that many restricted funds support activities directly related to the mission of an organization: exhibitions and educational programming, acquisitions to grow the permanent collection, and object conservation and digitization are all popular subjects of endowment restrictions. In addition to these mission-direct activities, endowments may be created to support capital needs, such as property maintenance, infrastructural systems upgrades, and technology needs. Such endowment gifts are not as common but are fundamental to the general health of the organization. It is important for staff to keep in mind not only funding terms but also their relationship to the organizational mission.

Mission is increasingly a point of reference for funders since 2017, when the Financial Accounting Standards Board (FASB), which oversees accounting standards in the United States, updated its regulations that stipulate that all nonprofits complete a statement of functional expenses as part of the annual financial report.[1] Unlike the statement of financial position, the statement of financial activities, and the statement of cash flows, this statement is designed to record the activity of an organization according to its mission relevance. As you can see from the sample (figure 3.3) provided from the Florence Griswold Museum in Old Lyme, Connecticut, the statement of functional expenses distinguishes between program services, which supports the mission of the organization, and supporting services, which does not benefit the mission but serves administration, like management and fundraising.

Since endowments are a permanently restricted asset and their use is recorded generally, they are not subject to this nuance in the financial report. So why mention it? Because as mission relevance grows as a means for evaluation of spending and operational activities, we should anticipate that even individual donors will expect to see mission relevance in their endowment terms and reports. Though donor management is the purview of the development team and typically not under the umbrella of financial management, savvy finance professionals will consider how mission relevance can be tracked and accounted for if needed.

Endowments and other institutional funds play a crucial role in terms of the current understanding of financial health and mission work, but also serve a purpose in considerations of the future of an organization. Museums undergo regular strategic planning, typically every three to five years, a process that should include both staff and trustees. Critical in these conversations is the understanding of how contributions, earned income, *and* endowments may evolve to serve the organization in the coming years. Discussions concerning multiyear planning activities should include endowments as a benefit of planned giving, and their use in supporting the future of the organization, especially as it relates to mission activation. Furthermore, consider if the institutional direction shifts enough that donors who have already committed funds to endowments should be notified, if only to assure mutual understanding regarding future use of the funds or if a restructuring of fund terms are to be addressed.

As board and staff members conceptualize the future of an organization, there are certain needs that are addressed. Will there be the need for a building expansion? How will we need to grow the staff to accommodate operational needs? In what ways do we expect to grow capacity and to be able to handle that growth? As will be addressed more fully in chapter 4, astute organizations build endowment campaigns into capital campaigns, intended to grow endowments to distribute more funds annually to meet additional operating needs. And from a practical perspective, consider the logistics of capital projects and the potential need to close an organization to the public for a period of time, which would negatively impact earned revenue opportunities. Endowments can provide essential support to offset

	Program Services				Supporting Services		
	Collections and Exhibits	Visitor Services	Educational Programs	Total Program Services	Administration	Development and Membership	Total
Salaries and wages	$ 220,160	$ 272,905	$ 205,106	$ 698,171	$ 267,899	$ 173,985	$ 1,140,055
Employee benefits	23,576	13,798	29,184	66,558	49,469	13,009	129,036
Payroll taxes	14,019	17,414	12,152	43,585	32,645	13,369	89,599
Facilities	98,429	214,729	86,738	399,896	85,817	85,723	571,436
Depreciation	173,899	188,080	25,438	397,417	31,282	10,550	439,249
Printing, publication and promotion	96,866	94,180	12,743	203,789	402	40,267	244,478
Contract services			41,488	41,488	37,601	48,954	128,043
Acquisition expense	277,321			277,321			277,321
Supplies	8,342	4,079	30,829	43,250	5,916	12,211	61,377
Travel and vehicle expense	54,536	3,833	17,358	75,727	13,171	1,013	89,911
Maintenance and repair	29,023	31,900		60,923			60,923
Equipment, licenses and fees						34,060	34,060
Miscellaneous	51,242		29,002	80,244	12,327	22,044	114,615
Postage and shipping	2,790	2,837	2,790	8,417	5,581	14,028	28,026
Membership dues		3,357		3,357		7,554	10,911
Interest expense					1,513		1,513
Total Expenses	$ 1,050,203	$ 857,112	$ 492,828	$ 2,400,143	$ 543,623	$ 478,787	$ 3,420,553

The accompanying notes are an integral part of the financial statements

Figure 3.3. Florence Griswold Museum statement of functional expenses. Courtesy of the Florence Griswold Museum.

such diminished income. The inclusion of endowment planning allows organizations to grow their asset base and their infrastructure as they grow their footprint, both during times of active change and in anticipation of future growth.

* * * * *

CASE STUDY: THE WOODLAWN MUSEUM
ELLSWORTH, MAINE

Mission: Woodlawn nurtures curiosity and a sense of place by promoting Downeast Maine's cultural heritage and offering diverse educational and recreational experiences.

The Woodlawn Museum, located adjacent to Acadia National Park in Downeast Maine, originated as the Hancock County Trustees of Public Reservations and was founded by a group of concerned citizens in response to the lumber economy and increasing private land use along the coast. The trustees preserved thousands of acres on Mount Desert Island, which was donated to the federal government and ultimately served as the basis for Acadia National Park. In 1929, the trustees received a bequest from donor George Nixon Black Jr. in the form of an 1820s-era house constructed by his ancestor Colonel John Black, as well as a collection of furnishings and decorative objects original to the house and belonging to the Black family.

Figure 3.4. The Woodlawn Museum. Courtesy of Joshua Torrance.

Today, Woodlawn is a 180-acre property that consists of a museum, garden, and park. Outbuildings that originally served as a carriage barn and a sleigh barn have been transformed into interpretive and program spaces, and a community garden was added to complement the formal garden designed in the Colonial Revival style in 1903. The organization was run by volunteers until 2000, when the organization hired Joshua Torrance as their inaugural executive director.

Upon his arrival, Torrance reviewed the financial assets of the organization, which included a gift to begin an endowment as part of George Nixon Black Jr.'s original 1929 bequest in the amount of $50,000. The original $50,000 was doubled by another gift of $50,000 in the 1950s, and together the gifts were intended to support the maintenance and care of the property. A four-year series of capital campaigns followed, and the first campaign, initiated in 2002, exceeded its goal of $1.1 million and included support for operations, preservation, and the endowment. By 2006, an additional $400,000 had been raised specifically for the endowment and with the goal to provide long-term and sustainable financial support to Woodlawn.

Woodlawn has benefited since 2006 from additions to the endowment, including $120,000 of proceeds from the sale of a Civil War era photo album deemed irrelevant to the permanent collection, which now funds collections conservation. Today, the endowment is valued at more than $3 million, with funds mainly available for unrestricted use and the two funds for capital needs and collections care. The policies are regularly reviewed by the board of trustees, including those relevant to the organization's endowment use, gift acceptance, and donor intent. Guided by the fiscally conservative policy articulated in the original 1929 bequest, Woodlawn does not use the total return on endowment investments, which would include appreciation or market gains, but only a calculation of interest earned. This policy prioritizes growth of the endowment corpus and, though Torrance acknowledges that the policy is dependent on market fluctuations, such modest regular use allows for maximum growth of the funds at a faster rate than if according to a set distribution rate per year.

Torrance departed Woodlawn in early 2020, and in his almost twenty years at the helm, he established financial policies and grew the endowment to such an extent that the organization can rely on its endowment for operating support while also consistently growing its value. A new capital campaign was launched in 2017, from which 20 percent of every dollar directly supports the endowment and the other 80 percent directly supports campaign and capital needs. Given this approach, Woodlawn demonstrates its commitment to building capacity and endowment.

What Can We Learn?

- *The establishment of procedures to ensure strong oversight of the endowment and other funds is essential.* The financial policies in place at Woodlawn rely on internal communication between staff and trustees, and consistent and transparent messaging to donors. The policies dictate the parameters of gift acceptance, which allow for more transparent messaging the donors.

- *Torrance offers that the endowment growth was done with the guidance from adept outside financial managers.* While some organizations may be attracted to low-cost alternatives to traditional endowment management, such as simply investing in mutual funds to avoid fees, both the prioritization of fund performance, as well as the fiduciary liability that lies with the trustees, should be considered.

★ ★ ★ ★ ★

THE DYNAMISM OF ENDOWMENTS

We have spent some time talking about managing endowments as a stream of operating support as well as the utility of endowments in funding special projects and planning. There is a certain dynamism to endowments, from internal and external circumstances. Externally, the market value determines the value of the endowments. Chapter 2 noted that the volatility of the market impacts the endowment based on how the spending rate is calculated, but even the most insulated of endowments are, fundamentally, investments that are respondent to the global economy. When the value of funds decreases, the corresponding distribution to the organization available for use also decreases.

Internal activities also dictate the health and accessibility of endowment funds. In addition to policy structures that articulate terms for endowment use and spending, we see that the utility of endowments is largely based on internal management and the division of endowments between operational use, projects and special needs, and in response to organizational change, capacity, and need. These interrelated activities are not independent of each other and function under a single institutional vision and resource base. We can see that endowment management requires consistent attention, which is vital to long-term financial health and in preparation for institutional change.

★ ★ ★ ★ ★

CASE STUDY: ECHO, LEAHY CENTER FOR LAKE CHAMPLAIN
BURLINGTON, VERMONT

Mission: ECHO inspires and engages families in the joy of scientific discovery, wonder of nature, and care of Lake Champlain.

Incorporated in 1995, the science and nature museum ECHO was in a temporary space until its building opened to the public in 2003. The facility is notable as the

Figure 3.5. ECHO, Leahy Center for Lake Champlain.
Courtesy of ECHO.

first LEED-certified (Leadership in Energy and Environmental Design) building in Vermont, and the only lake aquarium in the country to hold such a distinction. ECHO (Ecology, Culture, History, and Opportunities for Environmental Steward-ship) houses more than seventy varieties of fish, amphibians, invertebrates, and reptiles. In addition to its LEED-certified building, ECHO's 2.2-acre site hosts the Lake Champlain Navy Memorial, the University of Vermont's Rubenstein Ecosys-tem Science Laboratory, and the Lake Champlain Basin Program Resource Room. Named for Senator Patrick Leahy of Vermont, to honor his commitment to the sus-tainability of the Lake Champlain River Basin, ECHO, Leahy Center for Lake Cham-plain hosts living and natural history collections, special exhibition installations, and the Northfield Savings Bank 3-D Theatre.

ECHO maintains a staff of approximately 27 employees and 175 volunteers, and as of 2019 functioned on a budget of $3.5 million. Its endowment is valued at $8 million, all of which is formally unrestricted. Of the endowment, $7 million is invested via the Vermont Community Foundation, and the remainder with a private investment firm. ECHO's investment committee meets quarterly to review perfor-mance reports from the Community Foundation and the investment firm, a system that has been in place since 2015 when the investment portfolio and procedures were reviewed. At that time, the endowment was valued at $3.5 million and though the Community Foundation had been an obvious choice of investment partner, the board and staff of ECHO sought another option given the complex structure of the Foundation, the difficulty in withdrawing funds, and most importantly, the fact that until 2015, the Community Foundation would assume invested funds on their own books—meaning that ECHO's own endowment would not be listed as a propri-etary asset. Once the Community Foundation revised its structure, the investment committee of ECHO approved a partnership with the foundation. The Community

Foundation's commitment to investing in socially and environmentally conscious options also motivated the change (see chapter 5 for a discussion of ESG investing). Concurrent with the transition of the majority of ECHO's endowment to the stewardship of the Community Foundation, the investment of $1 million with a private firm allows for a certain degree of control on behalf of ECHO, as well as greater and more immediate access to funds.

ECHO's endowment policy, which was also drafted in 2015, allows for a maximum of 4 percent of the endowment to be distributed for current use. Interestingly, ECHO uses none of its endowment to support operations; instead, the funds are board-designated to support specific programs: the Leahy Fellows, an annual internship program, and capital needs. Phelan Fretz, executive director of ECHO, explains that this use structure reflects ECHO's prioritization of endowment growth. Since its inception, ECHO has enjoyed a high level of federal funding. Recognizing that government support is not certain in the future, the leadership of ECHO has a goal to expand its endowment to $12 million by 2024, at which point the distribution would partially underwrite operations. Individual support via planned giving agreements, as well as annual operating surpluses, are the two major forms of funding the endowment expansion.

Until ECHO crosses the $12 million threshold, the organization will continue to use its endowment only at the discretion of the board, and capital expenditures are a perfect fit. As Fretz comments, the maintenance of a LEED-certified building requires a high degree of stewardship, and the efficiency of its energy profile is a top priority. While many capital projects can receive support from donors, other time-sensitive needs are less appealing to the general public. The facility is now almost twenty years old, and many systems require upgrades or full replacement. Responsiveness to changing technology is, in fact, a mandate of LEED-certified buildings, and their costs are often offset by long-term financial benefits. The installation of solar panels, for instance, will ultimately net ECHO $50,000 in energy savings every year. In using the endowment for special purposes until an internally designated threshold is reached for operational use, ECHO assures that it is meeting its most pressing and mission-relevant needs while planning for its future.

What Can We Learn?

- *Consider mission relevance. ECHO is a site dedicated to environmental accountability and ecological awareness.* In its use of the endowment to support an internship program and LEED compliance, the site is actively attending to its mission of education and ecological conservation.
- *Fretz notes that the regular discussion of capital needs serves to educate board members and donors about the needs of the site.* He encourages all to consider strategic asset management and long-term planning, unifying institutional direction and a collective understanding of resources.

* * * * *

ENDOWMENTS AND INSTITUTIONAL VULNERABILITY

Thus far, our discussion has focused on the use of endowments for operations, projects and special needs, and planning. But what about when the institution is faced with unexpected problems? In concert with the board, the financial staff should keep in mind certain action steps when dealing with institutional vulnerabilities or crises, which can be caused by a variety of factors. Internal instability, whether expected or not, can cause a crisis situation. Leadership transitions or capital project management can be exciting times of institutional evolution that can cause financial instability if managed incorrectly. Other less welcome circumstances, such as corruption, fraud, or legal issues—such as lawsuits and consequent settlements due not covered by insurance—can also create institutional vulnerability. The creation of crisis conditions can happen through improper management, such as erroneous institutional scaling of operations, inaccurate income projections, or incorrect expense assumptions. Something as simple as major property damage due to a weather event can cause a financial crisis without sufficient insurance coverage or cash reserves to accommodate urgent repair costs.

Dealing with internal challenges and changes are one form of institutional vulnerability, and crisis can also be caused be external factors. The election of politicians who do not prioritize arts issues can lead to diminished funding at the local, state, and government levels. Policy revisions and updates to tax laws, such as the changing donation classifications in the Tax Cuts and Jobs Act of 2017, can produce donor reluctance and diminish individual giving. Downturns in the economy, such as the Great Recession in 2009, can negatively impact both the general philanthropic climate as well as investment returns, specifically the value of endowment funds and subsequent distributions.

The above situations are all possible scenarios that a professional will face in his or her museum career. Such conditions, while unwelcome, do not have to be fatal to an organization provided that an organization takes calculated steps to mitigate crisis.

Sequential Financial Planning: A Response to Crisis

Whether caused by internal or external factors, crises require specific actions to be taken to counteract the negative impact of volatile circumstances. Disaster planning and emergency preparedness resources often only address on-site accidents or mishaps, actionable responses to ensure professional reactions, and documentation. When considering extended crises, including those that may not be as easily attended to or are out of organization control—like a pandemic—different measures must be enacted to protect the organization.

A situation such as the 2020 pandemic is without a defined structure or conclusive timeframe, which can cause frustration and uncertainty. *Sequential financial planning* is a process I recommend for review of external and internal resources during a crisis; it is designed to protect and prioritize core assets, though does not exclude their access if necessary for institutional survival. I call this process *sequential* because the recommended actions progress in terms of invasion of core assets, including and concluding with a collections review. These recommendations are distinct from regular operating and financial oversight protocols, and are designed to be utilized when the future of an institution is at risk.

Relief Funding

When a financial crisis is motivated by a widespread situation, such as a pandemic and subsequent economic upheaval, relief funding may be available, as was the case in 2020. The hasty introduction of such funds can often mean inherent problems in funding structures at the federal level—such as relief offered in the form of multi-million dollar packages to large businesses, politicization of relief in the context of a capitalist economy, or the exclusion of tribal organizations—but the support offered in relief funding packages can be essential in cash flow management. Relief funding options such as Economic Impact Disaster Loans, the Payroll Protection Program, and the Main Street Lending Program provided vital liquidity to businesses facing devastating losses due to closure during the pandemic. Depending on the program, the funding may be totally or partially forgiven, or a low-interest loan to be repaid according to a predetermined schedule. Such programs may be offered at the federal level and/or granted at state and local levels, by public or private agencies, and serve as an effective first-line response to economic crisis.

Operational Activity Expectations

Whether or not relief funding is available at any stage of a protracted crisis situation, an institution must review its operations and revise activity expectations accordingly. The operating budget is the most obvious place to begin an activity review, and its revision will need to receive board approval. This allows for a discussion and mutual understanding of resources between board members and staff and is an important topic of conversation during a challenging period for an institution. When reviewing the annual budget, one must evaluate the likelihood of income sources, realistically scaling back expectations and accounting for relief funding, if awarded. A long closure, for instance, will impact earned revenue typically garnered through admissions and program attendance. The execution of a capital campaign may impact both earnings if a closure is necessary, as well as contributions that may be restricted to project expenses.

The evaluation of expenses is integral to a revision of activity expectations, and should be executed judiciously. Too often, institutions drastically reduce salaries and wages via pay reductions or the elimination of positions. While such an action will reduce expenses, it also reduces staff capacity, which can be an invaluable asset during a crisis. A close reading of expenditures can also yield cost savings in the elimination of operational inefficiencies and the retirement of programs unfeasible during a crisis. If you listen to your audiences during a crisis, there may be opportunities to suspend programs that were nearing their natural lifecycle anyway.

In addition to the revision of the annual operating budget, constant attention to resources during a time of financial instability is essential. The building of scenarios allows an organization to plan for its future needs, and determine its financial position as a crisis may continue. Will the organization be up and running in three months? In a year? If not able to function at full capacity, how many staff can we carry through the crisis? If we must close for a public health crisis and reopen gradually, how many visitors can we accommodate at any given time? Twenty-five percent of our average? Fifty percent? Reviewing such situations can allow a museum to determine its cash position at any time and to utilize cash flow projections to enact an appropriate response. Such exercises, which can be done frequently, are a worthwhile complement to a revised annual budget and to navigate a crisis with agility.

Cash Resources

Concurrent with the review of operational activity, an organization is well served in the review of its available cash resources, such as monies available in unrestricted spend-down accounts or a reserve fund. Many organizations refer to their reserve fund as a "rainy day" fund; while it can serve as an important source of cash to meet a short-term need (such as a large contractual agreement fee for which funding is secured but not yet received), don't forget that rainy day. A crisis situation is one in which accessible cash reserves could make the difference between making payroll or not, even for the largest institutions. Such unrestricted funds can be rebuilt, and can even serve as grounds for a campaign directed to offset operating losses or prepare the organization for future uncertainty. Furthermore, the evaluation and potential access of a reserve fund provides another valuable point of contact with board members to ensure proper use of such funds and may also be required by agencies in an application for relief funding, or a bank if a line of credit is sought.

Credit-Based Options

When dealing with long-term crises, loan programs and lines of credit are a valuable option, though less preferable than external relief funding options or use of institutional cash reserves. Though interest rates should be amenable for nonprofit organizations, and particularly tenable during times of economic instability, it is wise to consider the feasibility of increasing institutional debt load during an open-ended period of uncertainty. Increasing debt, particularly when facing a crisis, negates any cost efficiencies earned during the budget review and puts the organization in a more vulnerable financial position moving forward.

Institutional Funds

An organization has reviewed relief options, operational activities, its cash reserves, and potential credit-based options, and still finds itself in need of support in order to sustain operations. If an organization holds an endowment, one must remember that it is held in the public trust, for budgetary stability and review of its use during a crisis handled carefully. While each endowment is different, there is a way to consider use of the endowment during a crisis. The first is to approve a short-term adaption of the distribution rate to free funds for immediate use. As we know, the recommended endowment distribution rate for museums is between 4 and 5 percent of fund value. A short-term amendment of the distribution policy requires board approval and disclosure to auditors upon the close of the fiscal year, but is an option. Assuming an institution's spending rate is within a healthy range, such a change can be made with few long-term implications.

In order to maintain the health of the endowment, an organization would want to conserve the corpus and to ensure compliance with all restrictions placed on the gift when made by the donor. Should the organization be in such a state that the security of all assets is vulnerable, it is necessary to review gift terms with donors to consider alternate use of endowments and other restricted funds. Some donors may be amenable to changing their restriction terms or to fully unrestricting past or current contributions and pledges in order to maintain operations. In any case, such communication must be executed and documented. If donor restrictions are revised, or should the organization face such a situation in which they judge no choice but to further invade the endowment, the state attorney general should be consulted.

The discussion of financial management and endowments during times of institutional vulnerability is a relevant one in a climate of crisis and relates to the larger topic of financial sustainability. As nonprofit professionals, we recognize the value of sound financial management as an important best practice in any business; as museum professionals, we are hosting more conversations about resource management and financial sustainability than ever before, even predating the 2020 COVID-19 pandemic. In 2019, the American Alliance of Museums' (AAM) annual meeting included financial sustainability as a major conference theme, and in 2019, AAM published "TrendsWatch: The Future of Financial Sustainability" via its Center for the Future of Museums.[2] AAM has focused its national spotlight on financial issues as an ongoing strategic priority, with attention given to understanding income streams, government support, contributions, and financial capital and assets.

The topic of money is certainly not a new one in our field. So why is it currently garnering so much attention? There are a number of hypotheses: the overabundance of small organizations in our field that are incredibly vulnerable to market fluctuations, the increasing professionalization and growing menu of arts administrations programs, or even the simple realization that finance is a basic management function—the better a person understands it, the more attractive that individual may be as a potential leader. Whatever personal and contextual motivations may exist for our collective transition to finally and actively embrace financial stewardship as a cornerstone of strong museum oversight, we must be sure to make this conversation a productive one. When we discuss sound financial management, we often and erroneously reduce our interests to dollars and cents: the bottom line. While the centrality of income and expenses, and assets and liabilities can never be overstated, we must also consider astute management of all resources: tangible, capital, and human assets, as well as financial ones. In this way, we can best attend to finance as a component of strong operational oversight and better comprehend difficult decisions in challenging circumstances.

* * * * *

ISSUES IN THE FIELD: DIPPING INTO THE ENDOWMENT

A common discussion during times of institutional change and a difficult economic climate is that of dipping into the endowment, as it is commonly known, which essentially means taking more than the annual distribution rate allows and potentially invading the corpus of the fund. As noted, the spend policy is that which establishes the amount of the fund available to support institutional operations or special initiatives as fund restrictions allow. This policy, which is subject to board approval, can be amended when needed, and adapted to meet extenuating circumstances if warranted, but should always be heeded.

Invading the endowment should be an extremely rare occurrence and is generally discouraged. Why? For a number of reasons: most importantly, the invasion of the endowment corpus may be in violation of the donor agreement and may place the endowment value underwater (below the value of the original gift), which can endanger an organization's 501(c)(3) tax-exempt status. Additionally, invading the corpus prohibits healthy endowment growth and allows for poor planning; rather than attending to weak contributions or underperforming earned income streams, plugging operating losses from the endowment obscures the ability to address organizational weaknesses. This is particularly sensitive for smaller institutions, many of which have only a couple of months of working capital on hand in easily accessible reserves and may consider invasion of the endowment to be a necessary measure.[3] Without endowment coffers overflowing with funds, the invasion of the endowment will diminish its value swiftly.

Regardless of endowment size, prudent management is a necessity. Most states prohibit or strongly discourage the use of funds depreciated beyond their historic value or in violation of endowment terms as set by the donor, which violates donor intent and endanger tax-exempt status. Furthermore, most advice—which is reiterated in this chapter—is to exhaust reserves before even considering accessing an endowment beyond the regular distribution. A law passed in 2006 provides advisement on how to judiciously adapt an endowment usage during difficult circumstances. Called the Uniform Prudential Management of Institutional Funds Act (UPMIFA), the law has passed in forty-nine states and the District of Columbia (not Pennsylvania, which has its own stringent safeguards in place), and "lets people dip into a fund—even if it has fallen below its historic dollar value—as long as they're prudent in their spending and make preservation of the endowment's assets their top investment priority."[4] Should an organization face a potential dip into their endowment, consider a review of the UPMIFA terms and any other state guidelines with the office of the state attorney general before taking action, as well as the steps that can be taken to avoid disruption of the endowment corpus unless in truly unavoidable circumstances.

* * * * *

CONCLUSION

This chapter has addressed the role of financial management in endowment administration, highlighting the importance of strong institutional policies. A commitment to procedure in practice from endowment planning, through execution, and in planning, allows for active endowment management. Endowments are in many ways a living activity, and the funds require consistent stewardship from staff, trustees, and outside advisors.

Endowment management can prove challenging, not least of all because the returns on endowment work are long-term and benefit the future of an institution, not necessarily its present. Christopher Bedford, director of the Baltimore Museum of Art, explains that "building endowment is slow and arduous . . . it can sometimes feel you are raising millions and aren't seeing dividends."[5] Keep in mind that this lamentation comes from a director who has increased his endowment more than 40 percent in a little more than five years.

Many "successful" museum endowments are measured as such by purely internal means. Spend policies, terms, the dynamics between restricted and unrestricted use—much of this is internally determined by board and staff. There is not necessarily a "right" amount of endowment to use in supporting the operation: as we have seen in this chapter, museums vary their use policies according to their needs. Many organizations will have a quarter or a third of their operating budget supported via the endowment, others will have none at all. Of the massive operating budget of the Guggenheim, for a large-scale reference, only 5 percent is supported by the endowment.[6]

Are endowments really inflexible?[7] Well, no. There are multiple ways to craft a spend policy, consider and review oversight in terms of mission relevance, and to navigate institutional change and external pressures. Chapter 4 will take this one step further and discuss endowments in terms of our giving options, the role of donor relations, and how to establish funds to best serve the institution and future purposes.

Key Points: What Have We Learned?

- Endowments are not rigid. The board, staff, and external fund managers can determine how to use endowment funds to meet operating needs, support special initiatives, or plan for the future of an organization.
- Endowments are not a panacea. Consider the context for endowment spending during crisis moments and in sequence with other opportunities to secure financial health and maintain solvency.

NOTES

1. Tom Brean and Dennis Monroe, "FASB's Proposed Changes to the Design of Non-profit Financial Statements and What It Means for Your Museum," *American Alliance of Museums*, January 2, 2016, https://www.aam-us.org/2016/01/02/fasbs-proposed-changes-to-the-design-of-nonprofit-financial-statements-and-what-it-may-mean-to-your-museum/.
2. "TrendsWatch: The Future of Financial Sustainability," *American Alliance of Museums*, 2019.
3. Aileen Kwun, "Dipping into Endowments?" *DVDL*, March 30, 2020, https://dvdl.co/dipping-into-endowments/.
4. Terrie Temkin, "Can You Tap into Your Endowments During a Downturn," *Nonprofit World* 27, no. 4 (July–August 2009): 4, https://www.snpo.org/members/Articles/Volume27/Issue4/V270404.pdf.
5. Amy Haimerl, "What Keeps US Art Museums Running—and How Might the Pandemic Change That?" *Art News*, March 3, 2021, https://www.artnews.com/art-news/news/united-states-art-museum-financing-1234584930/.
6. Haimerl, "What Keeps US Art Museums Running?"
7. Leslie Ramos, "Museums Must Rethink How They Use Their Endowments—Or They'll Struggle to Rebuild after This Crisis," *Apollo Magazine*, October 30, 2020, https://www.apollo-magazine.com/the-trouble-with-museum-endowments/.

4

The Outstretched Hand

THE ROLE OF ENDOWMENTS IN FUNDRAISING

The development department serves a variety of vital roles in the life of the museum, and is responsible for acting as the hub for contributed income. In the creation of meaningful and magnetic campaigns, regular annual fundraising appeals, and the stewardship of relationships with donors, the development office is critical in maintaining financial health as well as public prominence. As is the case with all fundraising needs, endowment support is a balancing act: responsive to the evolutionary moment of the institution and its current needs versus its future ones.

Since the advent of the modern endowment in American philanthropy, the considerations of funding current projects and long-term investments has been central to the discussions of endowments. Chapter 1 noted Julius Rosenwald, founder of Sears, who maligned that "all of this giving and receiving is proceeding without much, if any, attention to the underlying question whether perpetual endowments are desirable."[1] The sentiment that endowment gifts are a less "desirable" form of giving remains for many donors today, as well as many nonprofit administrators, who often prefer the immediacy of direct gifts for current purposes.

Yet as we know, endowments and direct gifts do not serve the same goals, but benefit an organization in fundamentally different, though complementary, ways. Such differences are key in how we manage these funds effectively, and how we communicate the distinction and benefits to potential donors. Consistent messaging of short-term and immediate needs as well as institutional vision and long-term objectives are key in establishing support. This chapter will address how to plan for, accept, and steward endowment donations, as well as how to cultivate and manage relevant donor relationships.

ENDOWMENT FUNDING AND CAMPAIGNS

When considering how to establish an endowment, many institutions will elect to start a fund with a formal campaign, or as a component of a larger comprehensive campaign. Comprehensive campaigns are those that are designed to raise funds for operational support and capacity-building as well as physical needs, as opposed to capital campaigns that are designed to fund a specific need (usually to fund capital projects, expansions, and restoration) within a certain timeframe. Since growing capacity is a major focus of a comprehensive campaign and the thrust of endowment support, consider that donor relations are key, as is messaging organizational stability. Donors are investors in an institution, and no one wants to make an unsound investment.

When to Launch an Endowment Campaign

Gifts to an endowment are a long-term investment, both literally and figuratively: the funds are designed to be invested and with a regular distribution to support the organization. A six-figure donation for immediate use may feel like winning the lottery; a similar donation to the endowment may act as an annual allowance to the organization for years to come. Before launching a formal endowment, remember that its benefits lend to the organization future sustainability. Immediate needs such as operations and additional funds that may be needed in case of business interruptions, must already be accommodated. Consider the following questions when reflecting on the timing of an endowment campaign:

- Do you have and consistently receive enough income to support your operating needs at its current level?
- Can you identify areas of potential growth and, if funds were made available, how to sustainably manage capacity growth?
- Is your development department equipped both in terms of human resources and technology to process endowment gifts?
- Do you have an established relationship with outside investment firms who can manage such gifts and an endowment portfolio?
- Do you have a reserve fund to meet current needs or unforeseen circumstances?
- Do you consider your top priority to be investment in the future rather than easily accessible cash?

These are all areas to reflect upon before you solicit endowment gifts; the more questions you can answer "yes" to, the better position you are in to begin an endowment campaign.

ENDOWMENTS AND DONOR MESSAGING

Since capacity-building and financial health are at the heart of endowment support, think about what would be most essential in "scaling up" the organization: while we recognize that an endowment push has the best chances when an organization maintains a strong pool of donors and can consistently meet its needs at its current level, endowment fundraising serves an organization in a state of growth and evolution. Endowment support that is unrestricted is always ideal, but giving donors a sense of potential avenues of support can also hold appeal. One area that is popular with donors is that of strengthening the administration, as in the creation of new staff positions, endowing existing leadership titles, or the expansion of mission-relevant programs and initiatives. Another popular track is in the growth of the organizational infrastructure, which often intersects with capital expansion, but can just as easily be promoted as the underwriting of enhancements to utilities and systems needs, technology, and security upgrades.

And what is the overarching theme when speaking to donors about endowments? The future. When requesting endowment support, one is literally issuing an invitation to invest in the vision of an organization. Such areas of development are often identified during strategic planning or campaign readiness phases, which can provide evidence of such needs and cost analyses for conversations with donors. Specific areas for development, such as ecological sustainability, financial health, technology and security, and risk aversion may be addressed in institutional planning or feasibility conversations. Donors appreciate data and confident planning, to be sure; just as much, they also value being on the inside track and playing a major part in driving an organization forward.

The magnetism of contributing to an organization's future is not, however, of appeal to all current or prospective donors. Some donors may be new to your community, or to philanthropy in general, and will be most comfortable giving via more modest means as they increase familiarity with the process and your core values. It is also reasonable to consider how we guide donors to support our institutions. We recognize that a gift of $250 is welcome to meet an annual fundraising goal, though will have nominal impact on building an endowment. The mutual understanding of donor intent and institutional benefit is critical to healthy donor relationships, and certainly underscore the best fundraising planning. By maintaining consistent stewardship of donors and clarity of goals and organizational needs at every giving level, the donor who gives $250 each year could evolve into a $10,000 benefactor.

GIFT ACCEPTANCE POLICIES AND PROCEDURES

Important in donor engagement is the ability to welcome gifts and to process them according to established, compliant, and transparent procedures. I recommend the creation and regular review of specific resources that are relevant to multiple fundraising activities, inclusive of endowment support:

- *Gift acceptance policy.* The gift acceptance policy is the institution's manual for how gifts are accepted and processed. The policy should include language addressing general guidelines that are applicable to all gift transactions, as well as the definition of gift categories and appeals. Procedures for different gift types should be articulated, including those related to cash, stocks and bonds, tangible gifts, or gifts to the collection, such as artwork. See figure 4.1.

GIFT POLICIES AND PROCEDURES
The ABC Museum

Mission Statement:

Highlights:

The purpose of this document is to provide the Board of Trustees and the professional staff of the ABC Museum with charitable gift acceptance policies and guidelines.

The Museum will seek advice of qualified legal and financial counsel whenever appropriate.

Any donor planning on making a substantial gift to the ABC Museum should be advised to review the federal and state tax consequences of the proposed gift with his or her own tax advisor before completing the gift.

The Board of Trustees has the right to refuse gifts or contributions that do not enhance, promote or ensure the mission of the ABC Museum and the long-range viability of the institution.

Accepted and approved by the Board of Trustees

(NEWLY ACCEPTED DATE)

Figure 4.1. Sample gift acceptance policy. Courtesy of Rebekah Beaulieu.

Gifts to the ABC Museum will be accepted for purposes consistent with the museum's mission. All donors to the ABC Museum will be urged to support the priorities of the museum. Final authority for gift acceptance rests with the Director and the Board of Trustees, in consultation with the Director of Development. The Collections Management Policy covers gifts of works of art.

The following policies seek to assure that all gifts will provide maximum benefit to the museum, to the donor, and the donor's heirs. Except where stated otherwise, these policies are intended as guidelines. The ABC Museum will seek the advice of qualified legal and financial counsel when appropriate. Donors are always encouraged to consult with their own legal and financial advisors when considering special gifts.

I.   **General Guidelines**

Donors are encouraged to make outright cash gifts. However, programs have been developed to accommodate a variety of planned giving objectives (See "Planned Giving" policy below).

Commitments to the museum may be made through outright gifts, or pledges payable, preferably, over not more than a five-year period. Exceptions, which would extend the payment period beyond five years, require initial approval by the Director of Development and the Director. Pledges are effective on the day in which proper documentation is signed and received by the museum (see "Gift Documentation" below).

Gifts may include:
- Cash or cash equivalents
- Securities or other types of appreciated assets
- All forms of charitable remainder trusts, gift annuities, and life estates
- Insurance (cash values for fully assigned policies)

- Works of Art
- Real and personal property, equipment, and other gifts-in-kind
- Corporate, federal, state, and private matching funds

Donors making pledges documented in writing and scheduled for payment in full will be recognized in full at the time of the pledge.

The decision to write off a pledge will be made by the Director of Development, in consultation with the Director of Finance. (Note: The Director of Finance will report to the Investment Committee on write-offs and delinquent pledges. Efforts to obtain delinquent pledges will be coordinated and appropriately documented by the Development Department).

As a general rule, investment earnings on gifts will be excluded from gift counting. Subject to any donor restrictions, such earnings shall be applied to the museum's general purposes.

The Executive Committee of the Board and/or Campaign Leadership Committee (when appropriate and in effect) is responsible for setting guidelines and approving recommendations from the museum staff for the appropriate recognition of leadership gifts. All donors will be recognized in the Annual Report unless otherwise directed.

While benefits, especially tax and financial considerations, may accrue to donors in certain circumstances, the donor must have a "donative intent" as the primary motive for making a gift. Donative intent is the intention to give away something of value for the betterment of the museum.

The museum reserves the right not to accept any gifts and will not accept any gift that entails any violation of law or public policy. Gifts with significant restrictions that unduly burden the museum will be reviewed by the Director of Development in consultation with Museum Counsel and Director.

II.   Gift Documentation

Outright gifts and pledges require written documentation in the form of a gift agreement letter or correspondence confirming the donor's gift or pledge. Planned gifts require copies of trust/estate/gift documents.   Pledges will not be counted or entered without proper documentation. All gifts and pledges will be recorded in compliance with IRS regulations and FASB accounting standards.

3

Figure 4.1. (*Continued*)

Questions pertaining to specific gift acceptance policies and recognition guidelines shall be referred to the Director of Development.

III.   Standards of Conduct

The primary role of museum employees, with regard to gifts to the museum, is to inform, serve, guide, and assist individuals, families, and organizations in realizing their philanthropic objectives. Tax advice is for information purposes only, and donors should obtain their own independent attorneys, consultants, and tax advisors.   Employees, including consultants and advisors, shall be paid a salary, wage, or fee by the museum and shall never be compensated with a commission for obtaining such gifts.

The museum will not knowingly accept gifts that result in an unethical or illegal advantage to the donor or a third party.

All information obtained from or about donors and potential donors will be held in strict confidence by the museum, except as may be required by law. Requests for donor anonymity will be closely honored, except when in conflict with best practice or by law.

IV.   Gift Acceptance and Crediting

- **Cash/Credit Card**
  Cash and credit card payments will be credited to the donor at full current value on the date of the gift. The ABC Museum will absorb the gift processing fees as a cost of fundraising.

- **Publicly-Traded Securities**
  Gifts of readily marketable securities will be credited at the full fair market value based on the average of the high and low quoted selling price on the date of transfer to the museum. Shares of mutual funds will be credited at the net asset value of the shares on the transfer date.

  The museum's general policy is that securities will be sold immediately by the museum through its agent or representative. No employee or volunteer may make a commitment to a donor that a particular security will be held by the museum, unless otherwise authorized by the Director in consultation with the Director of Finance.

4

- **Closely-Held Securities**
Gifts of securities that are not publicly traded will be evaluated on a case-by-case basis by the Investment Committee. Acceptance of such a gift will be at the Investment Committee's discretion, following an evaluation of the conditions affecting the eventual sale of the securities. Such gifts will be credited at fair market value as determined by a qualified, independent appraiser retained and compensated by the donor. If restrictions are placed on the securities by the donor or by the terms of the securities themselves, acceptance of the gifts shall be subject to prior approval by the Investment Committee.

- **Matching Gifts**
Matching gifts received from organizations and corporations will be credited to the organization or company that makes the matching gift. The individual recommending the matching gift will receive recognition credit. The individual's giving record will reflect inclusion of the matching gift, although the gift itself will count only once in report totals. Matching gifts may be applied as payment towards an individual's pledge only if allowed by the matching organization. The matching gift will be used for the same purpose as the recommending donor's original gift, unless that use is prohibited by the matching gift organization's guidelines.

- **Gifts of Art**
Gifts of Art are governed by the museum's Collection Management Policy.

- **Gifts-in-Kind/Tangible Personal Property**
The museum welcomes gifts-in-kind, including intangible and tangible personal property, based upon the museum's determination of the immediate usefulness of the gift. This determination will be made by the Director of Development.

Gift credit will be provided on the basis of full fair market value of the gift at the time of the donation according to IRS guidelines. Donors may choose to designate the sale proceeds of gifts of personal property (net of all expenses) to a specific program, or to make an unrestricted gift in support of the museum.

- **Gifts of Real Estate**
Gifts of real estate may take the form of an outright gift of the donor's entire interest in the property, or the donor may wish to retain a life interest in the property. Whether the gift is of a present interest or the remainder interest, an independent appraisal is necessary, commissioned and paid for by the donor, for

5

Figure 4.1. (*Continued*)

both tax and gift counting purposes. Acceptance of a gift of real estate is subject to the prior approval by the Director, Director of Finance, and Director of Development, after consultation with Museum Counsel. All gifts of real estate must receive approval by the board after review and recommendation by the Executive Committee.

Donors of real estate will receive credit for the fair market value of the property, as determined by qualified, independent appraisal, at the time of the gift. Generally, gifts of real estate will be liquidated on the public market as soon as possible, rather than held and managed for investment purposes.

Gift real estate must be tested and be in conformity with state and federal laws, including EPA regulations, and the donor must provide satisfactory evidence of environmental compliance.

By and large, for the museum to enter into an agreement for a gift of property subject to retained life tenancy, the gift must meet these conditions: (1) the property must have a minimum value of $250,000 established by a qualified appraiser and (2) the tenants shall be age 65 or older.

Life tenancy contracts must include provisions stipulating that the tenant-donor is obligated to maintain the property, that the tenant-donor is financially responsible for its physical upkeep in all respects, that the tenant-donor pays all taxes on the property as well as necessary insurance, and that the tenant-donor does not encumber the property with debt of any kind.

Donors of split-interest or retained life estate will receive credit based on the present value of the gift. Such gifts will be counted equivalent to irrevocable planned gifts.

- **Restricted Gifts**
  Endowments
  Endowments provide funds which generate income from interest and investment performance and are intended to endure indefinitely. Gifts to the endowment are permanent and are strongly encouraged

  Minimum current value of $25,000 is required to establish a named endowed fund. Gift agreements shall specify that if any named endowment fund is not fully funded by the donor within a twelve-month period, the endowment may be allocated to an existing endowment fund used for a comparable purpose, or added to the unrestricted endowment at the discretion of the Board of Trustees with the approval of the Director.

<u>Restricted Funds</u>
Each year, the museum solicits support beyond operations for special exhibitions and other museum projects. Gifts for special projects (restricted gifts) shall be restricted for the purpose designated. For each special project, donors will be recognized in accordance with existing practice or as specified in the sponsorship agreement for such gifts, including credit for the project or program.

- **Planned Gifts**
  The ABC Museum encourages planned gifts that strengthen the financial resources of the museum in support of its mission. The acceptance of planned gifts by the museum is guided by the General Policies for Planned Gifts, as below.

V.   <u>Recognition Practices</u>
The ABC Museum will make accurate and timely acknowledgement of all its donors.

When appropriate, the museum may recognize its donors further in the following ways:

- **Naming Opportunities**
  The Museum offers opportunities which may be named in honor of a person or organization. The amount of the gift necessary to qualify for such naming opportunities commensurate with their location, visibility, scale, etc. The naming opportunities are managed and made available through the Director of Development. A gift agreement consistent with this policy shall be executed for gifts that include naming opportunities, detailing scope of the gift and the duration of the naming period.

  Naming opportunities will not be offered in recognition of donated artwork.

  Opportunities for naming include, but are not limited to:

  Galleries, courtyards, offices, meeting spaces, reception spaces, and other spaces of the museum's interior and exterior property.

7

Figure 4.1. (*Continued*)

The museum's preference and priority is to receive endowments in addition to gifts of capital whenever possible to support these named spaces. The duration of a naming period shall not exceed twenty-five (25) years, unless otherwise determined by the Board of Trustees in consultation with the Director.

Named spaces will be determined based on the value of cash gifts. Irrevocable planned gifts may also factor into the determination of appropriate naming opportunities. Revocable planned gifts or gifts of art cannot be used for naming opportunities.

- **Previously Designated/Named Spaces**
  The museum from time to time will determine the need to renovate or reconstruct existing museum spaces. If this affects a named space, the donor or his or her descendants whenever possible will be informed of the proposed changes to the space. For those with a term named space (25-years) still in effect, an alternate comparable named space will be offered, if necessary and to the extent practicable and otherwise consistent with this policy, for the remaining duration of the naming period.

- **Right of First Opportunity**
  Upon the expiration of the designated term for a named space, program, or otherwise, if the naming opportunity will be continued, the ABC Museum will, to the extent practicable and otherwise consistent with best practice and this policy, first offer the donor or the donor's family, if known, for ninety (90) days, the opportunity to renew the naming of such space, position, department or program on the same terms and conditions as the ABC Museum intended to offer other potential donors.

GENERAL POLICIES FOR PLANNED GIFTS

I. Promotion of Planned Giving

Deferred gifts maximize private philanthropic support for the ABC Museum by broadening the base of support and enabling donors to make larger gifts during their lifetimes than would otherwise be possible.

All members of the Development Committee, Director of Development, Director, and Trustees are encouraged to talk with prospective donors about deferred gifts. If a donor wishes to participate in a deferred gift plan, the donor should be encouraged to contact the Director of Development. It is critical that any volunteer or employee of the museum advocating for a planned gift be careful not to place him or herself in the position of serving as the legal, financial, or tax advisor to a donor. It is incumbent on the the donor to seek the independent advice of his or her attorney or advisors on all matters relating to a proposed gift or transaction.

The museum seeks to provide appropriate materials and information that will assist prospective donors in their consideration of a deferred gift plan. As a service to the donor and his/her advisors, the Director of Development may provide examples, calculations, sample documents, and other materials, provided

Figure 4.1. (*Continued*)

these are accompanied by a written statement that they are examples and that the donor must seek the advice of his/her own private counsel.

II.   Balancing Donor Interest and Museum Purpose

It is recognized that the solicitation, planning, and administration of a charitable gift is a complex process involving philanthropic, personal, financial, tax, and estate planning considerations. Representatives of the museum will work with donors and advisors to structure a gift that achieves a fair and proper balance between the interests of the donor and the purposes of the museum.

No planned gift contract, trust agreement, or commitment of any type shall be urged on a prospective donor which unduly benefits the museum at the expense of the donor's interest.

III.   Trusteeship

The choice of trustee in any gift planning trust document shall be at the discretion of the donor. Generally, the museum will not serve as Trustee but circumstances may arise when it agrees to do so at the request of a donor.

The museum shall execute no gift planning agreement involving the museum serving as trustee or as manager of the assets of a trust, or any other form of agreement involving a legal or financial commitment by the museum to a donor, without first seeking the advice of the museum's legal counsel, with ultimate decision by the Director.

IV.   Use of Legal and Financial Counsel

It is imperative that no planned gift agreement be urged upon a prospective donor unless the donor is advised and encouraged to discuss the agreement in detail with his/her own legal and financial advisor. The museum may provide referrals for legal, financial, and/or estate planning professionals to prospective donors and/or their advisors. The museum will not receive a fee for these referrals from any party. Referrals are neither an endorsement nor guarantee of prospective services or work product.

V.   Compensation

Compensation paid by the museum to professionals involved in any aspect of the creation of a planned gift shall be reasonable and proportional to the services rendered and consistent with standard business practices.

VI.   Donor Recognition

The ABC Museum's Lieutenant River Society was established in 1995 to recognize donors who have informed the museum of their intentions to make a bequest to the museum. The museum will respect any donor's wish to remain anonymous.

Realized planned gifts will be formally recognized upon maturity in the same manner as other gifts. In some instances, immediate recognition may be offered to donors for planned gifts that are irrevocable.

VII.   Planned Gift Acceptance

The museum accepts planned gifts that support the mission, vision, and strategic objectives of the institution. All proposed gifts will be reviewed to ensure accordance with the museum's general Gift Acceptance Policies. The museum reserves the right to refuse any planned gift which is deemed to not be in the best interests of the institution.

VIII.   Determination of Cash Bequests

All undesignated cash bequests shall be added to the museum's unrestricted endowment unless the Director recommends a different designation to the Finance Committee of the Board of Trustees.

IX.   Planned Giving Vehicles

• Bequests
A bequest is a testamentary gift stipulated in an individual's will or trust, usually in the form of cash, securities, real property, art and other forms of

Figure 4.1. (*Continued*)

personal property. Donors may name the museum as a specific or remainder beneficiary. Gifts may also be contingent, so that assets go to the museum only if the named primary beneficiary does not survive the donor. The appropriate means of naming the museum as a beneficiary is: The ABC Museum, Inc.

• Charitable Gift Annuities (immediate and deferred)

A charitable gift annuity is a contract between the donor and the museum in which the museum agrees to pay the donor/beneficiary a fixed income for life in exchange for a gift of cash or marketable securities. The level of income is dependent on the age of the beneficiary and the size of the gift. The museum follows recommended rates suggested by the American Council on Gift Annuities. The museum reserves the right to not accept real estate or tangible personal property for the purpose of funding gift annuities. The museum encourages annuity funding with cash and/or appreciated, publicly traded securities.

A deferred gift annuity is similar, except that the donor/beneficiary agrees to defer receiving the annuity income until some future date (often coinciding with retirement). This gift often appeals to younger donors who have high current income and need the benefit of a current tax deduction, but are also interested in providing for future income.

Annuitants must be aged 65 or older. The Museum will accept single life gift annuities only. The minimum gift to establish a gift annuity (immediate or deferred) is $25,000 for one life. Each annuity is a separate contract; no additions to an existing annuity may be made.

Annuity payments amounts will be rounded upward to ensure that each payment will be exactly the same amount. Payments will be made quarterly and will be mailed in time to arrive on the payment date as agreed upon between the museum and donor.

The full annuity gift will be admitted to a segregated gift annuity fund of the museum and will be maintained until the demise of the annuitant as stated in the agreement.

The gift annuity will be effective as noted on the gift annuity contract signed by the donor and a Museum representative upon receipt of a cash donation. In the case of a stock gift the charitable annuity will be effective on the date the Museum receives notice from the broker regarding stock transfer instructions.

Each donor will receive the Museum's charitable gift annuity disclosure statement and gift annuity (contract) agreement. The Museum reserves the right not to accept any particular type of property as payment to acquire a charitable gift annuity.

- **Retained Life Estate**

An individual can obtain a current charitable income, gift, and estate tax deduction for donating a gift of a remainder interest in his or her residence (a primary home, vacation home or farm) to the museum. The donor retains a life estate (for one or more lives or a term of years) and can continue to live on and use the property. The gift is made by executing and recording a deed and then transferring the remainder interest to the museum. Acceptance of a gift of real property is subject to the prior approval of the museum as detailed in the museum's General Policies for Gift Acceptance above. Real property will not be accepted unless the museum and the donor enter into an arrangement specifying the responsibilities of each party including taxes, insurance, and maintenance. The donor must obtain and pay for a qualified appraisal.

- **Life Insurance**

Life insurance is a strategy for donor wealth replacement and minimizing estate tax liability.

A gift of an insurance policy is a deferred giving device, which requires the assignment of the ownership of the policy to the museum, and continued premium payments by the donor (unless the policy is paid up). The donor may retain the ownership of the policy and designate the museum as the beneficiary, but there are no current charitable gift or tax deductions. The museum must be the absolute owner and beneficiary of the insurance policy in order for the donor to receive a current charitable gift deduction.

The gift may be in the form of a new policy or an existing policy. The policy may insure the donor, or the donor and another person, such as a spouse (i.e. a survivorship life policy). Premium payments may be made by the donor, or the donor may wish to give cash payments to the museum and allow it to make the premium payments. The museum will accept gifts of life insurance policies, but will ordinarily not make payments for premiums on such policies

Figure 4.1. (*Continued*)

the Museum receives notice from the broker regarding stock transfer instructions.

Each donor will receive the Museum's charitable gift annuity disclosure statement and gift annuity (contract) agreement. The Museum reserves the right not to accept any particular type of property as payment to acquire a charitable gift annuity.

- **Retained Life Estate**
An individual can obtain a current charitable income, gift, and estate tax deduction for donating a gift of a remainder interest in his or her residence (a primary home, vacation home or farm) to the museum. The donor retains a life estate (for one or more lives or a term of years) and can continue to live on and use the property. The gift is made by executing and recording a deed and then transferring the remainder interest to the museum. Acceptance of a gift of real property is subject to the prior approval of the museum as detailed in the museum's General Policies for Gift Acceptance above. Real property will not be accepted unless the museum and the donor enter into an arrangement specifying the responsibilities of each party including taxes, insurance, and maintenance. The donor must obtain and pay for a qualified appraisal.

- **Life Insurance**
Life insurance is a strategy for donor wealth replacement and minimizing estate tax liability.

A gift of an insurance policy is a deferred giving device, which requires the assignment of the ownership of the policy to the museum, and continued premium payments by the donor (unless the policy is paid up). The donor may retain the ownership of the policy and designate the museum as the beneficiary, but there are no current charitable gift or tax deductions. The museum must be the absolute owner and beneficiary of the insurance policy in order for the donor to receive a current charitable gift deduction.

The gift may be in the form of a new policy or an existing policy. The policy may insure the donor, or the donor and another person, such as a spouse (i.e. a survivorship life policy). Premium payments may be made by the donor, or the donor may wish to give cash payments to the museum and allow it to make the premium payments. The museum will accept gifts of life insurance policies, but will ordinarily not make payments for premiums on such policies unless the donor agrees to make a separate gift to cover the premium cost. When the insured dies, the life insurance proceeds are paid to the museum.

SUGGESTED WORDING FOR
GIFT INSTRUMENT BEQUESTS

I bequeath to the ABC Museum, Inc., of City, State (TAX ID) or its successors $ _____ to be used for its general charitable purposes.

I bequeath to the ABC Museum, Inc., of City, State (TAX ID) all the rest, residue and remainder of my estate to be used for its general charitable purposes.

I bequeath to the ABC Museum, Inc., of City, State (TAX ID), _____ percent (%) of my residuary estate to be used for its general charitable purposes.

Note: Restricted gifts should be clearly defined and stated in the bequest. The museum should note the donor's name and date the bequest was completed.

THE ABC MUSEUM
WIRE INSTRUCTIONS

Receiving Firm Information

Incoming Securities (STOCK TRANSFERS)

14

Figure 4.1. (*Continued*)

- *Pledge agreement.* Common for those giving to capital campaigns, comprehensive campaigns, or a large amount according to a schedule, the pledge agreement allows for installments to be made toward a stated amount over a period of time. The typical pledge agreement includes total donation amount, the date and terms of the gift agreement, and the anticipated payment installment schedule. Donor intent should be clearly stated, and language regarding potential amendment to the terms or intent of the gift included. (This is often the case in situations when legal status has changed, such as divorce or criminality.) See figure 4.2.

<<Date>>

Mr. John Smith
1 Main Street
Anytown, USA 01234

Dear John,

We are pleased to confirm our commitment of [amount in words] ($xxx,xxx.00) to the ABC Museum for (list of fund or purpose). This gift will be designated to (name of fund, annual fund, restricted, unrestricted, endowment, etc.) of the Museum. This letter confirms the terms of a verbal pledge which I made to the ABC Museum on (date of verbal pledge).

Recognizing that the Museum's Board of Trustees and Director will rely upon my pledge when making expenditures, entering into contracts, and engaging in other activities for the benefit of the Museum, and recognizing further that others have made and will make contributions to the Museum for like purposes, we hereby pledge in consideration thereof the sum of $xxx,xxx.00.

Our plan is to fund this gift over a (#) year period. The timing of the funding of the gift installments will be at our discretion, but we will complete the whole of the gift payment by (date). The pledge will be fulfilled by cash payments or gifts of marketable securities.

Although the funding of the gift is at our discretion, we recognize that timely payment is vital. We will consider the following to be a reasonable outline for payments:

By December 31, 2019 $xx,xxx to the <<Name of Fund>>
By December 31, 2020 $xx,xxx to the <<Name of Fund>>
By December 31, 2021 $xx,xxx to the <<Name of Fund>>

This pledge agreement may be altered or amended only by a subsequent agreement executed in writing by ourselves and the Museum. This pledge agreement shall be construed in accordance with and governed by the laws of the State of _____.

Figure 4.2. Sample pledge agreement. Courtesy of Rebekah Beaulieu.

(over)

It is understood that by naming the <<TBD>>, the ABC Museum reserves the right to revoke a naming of an endowed fund, building, or otherwise, if for any reason it presents risk or harm to the reputation of the Museum, or if the intent of a gift or the terms of a sponsorship associated with the naming cannot be fulfilled. Naming may be revoked by the Director with approval of the Director of Development and a majority vote of the Board of Trustees.

Please acknowledge your acceptance of my pledge in accordance with the terms herein described by signing and returning a copy of this letter to me.

_____   _____
Donor #1   Donor #2

Date _____

ABC Museum hereby accepts and acknowledges the foregoing pledge and accepts its terms as of the date written.

FOR ABC MUSEUM:

_____   _____
Director   Director of Development

Date _____

- *Naming agreement.* High-value gifts, such as those to name buildings in a capital campaign, or those to name endowment funds, are subject to a naming agreement. Such agreements detail the terms for the gift, including spending policies and gift use. For an endowment, such policies might include if the agreement should also include any restrictions on use or spending or if a spending threshold is in effect (and the fund is considered an endowment only after it has reached a certain amount). The agreement should also outline the expectations of the donor commitment and the staff and trustee responsibilities in terms of stewarding the funds. See figure 4.3.

[Named Fund]
Statement of Understanding

Purpose

The [name] Fund for the [purpose] (the "Fund") is a gift designed to support [purpose description] at the ABC Museum (the "Museum"). Income from endowment is used to secure the future and growth of the Museum. Private support designated for endowment is critical investment in the Museum's 21st century vision. It is inspirational to recognize the enduring impact made through the committed philanthropy of the Museum's donors, as well as those who are honored and memorialized through these endowed funds.

Administration

Expenditures of income from the [name] Fund for [purpose] will be administered by the Director of the Museum (the "Director") in consultation with the Board of Trustees, which may consult with or delegate to such other persons or committees as deemed appropriate within the intent of the Donor. As with other endowed funds, the Director and Director of Finance, in consultation with the Investment Committee of the Board of Trustees, will oversee this Fund in accordance with the endowment management, distribution, and utilization policies established by the Board of Trustees. These policies govern the investment of endowment funds and the distribution and utilization of endowment earnings for the purposes designated by the donors, including direct and associated costs incurred pursuant to those purposes. These policies may be revised by the Board of Trustees.

Funding

For the establishment of an endowed fund, the Museum will accept all appropriate receipts and gifts properly designated for this Fund, which, together with any additional contributions, memorials, bequests of cash or securities, or other personal or real property, shall be administered by the Museum as a part of its endowment pursuant to the Museum's management and investment policies. No distributions from this Fund may be made, and the earnings shall be accumulated, unless or until the endowed Fund's balance is $25,000 or greater. If the balance does not reach $25,000 within five (5) years from the date hereof, or if at least $5,000 in contributions in each year are not added to the balance within the 5-year period before reaching a $25,000 balance, then this Fund shall become part of the Museum's unrestricted endowment and be subject to its terms and conditions as set forth by the Board of Trustees.

(over)

Donor's Intent

Figure 4.3. Sample naming agreement. Courtesy of Rebekah Beaulieu.

The donor intends to fund the [name] Fund in the amount of [$ amount] to be paid in full, by installment or full amount, by [date].

Practicability and Naming Rights

In the event that the stated purpose of the [name] Fund for [purpose] becomes unreasonably burdensome, impossible or impracticable to carry out, as determined by the discretion of the Director and the Board of Trustees, then the Board of Trustees and Director, in their discretion, may select another purpose of the [name] Fund for [purpose] as nearly consistent as reasonably possible with the donor's original purpose.

[*Add if appropriate:* The Donor's generosity will be recognized by the Museum by [naming of building, program, materials, XYZ]. The ABC Museum reserves the right to remove or modify the recognition of the Donor or revoke a naming of an endowed fund, building or otherwise, if for any reason it presents risk or harm to the reputation of the Museum, or if the intent of a gift or the terms of a sponsorship associated with the naming cannot be fulfilled. Naming may be revoked by the Director with approval of the Director of Development and a majority vote of the Board of Trustees.

This Statement of Understanding shall be construed in accordance with and governed by the laws of the State of _____.

ABC Museum's Acceptance

The ABC Museum gratefully accepts the Donor's intention to establish the [name] Fund for [purpose].

All guidelines have been reviewed and are now accepted by:

ABC Museum: **Donor(s):**

_____   _____
Director   [Name]

_____   _____
Director of Development   [Name]

_____   _____
Date   Date

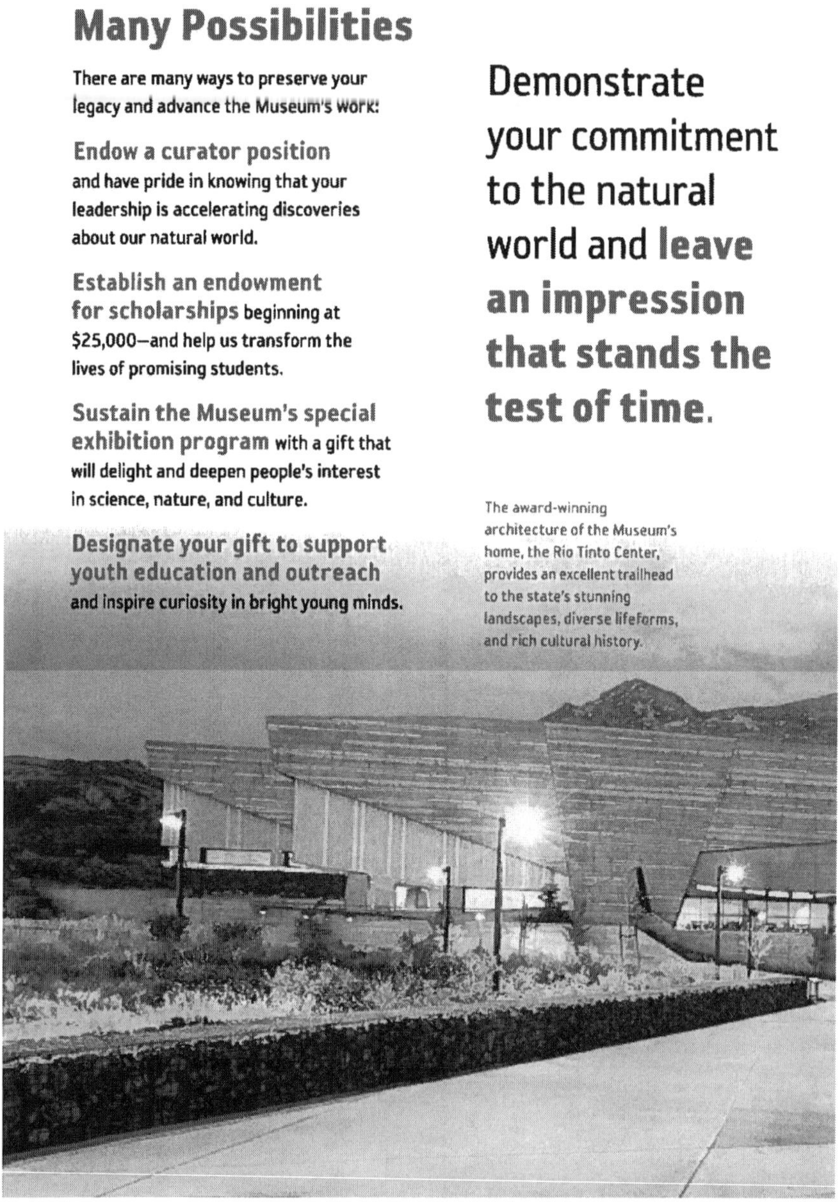

Many Possibilities

There are many ways to preserve your legacy and advance the Museum's work:

Endow a curator position and have pride in knowing that your leadership is accelerating discoveries about our natural world.

Establish an endowment for scholarships beginning at $25,000—and help us transform the lives of promising students.

Sustain the Museum's special exhibition program with a gift that will delight and deepen people's interest in science, nature, and culture.

Designate your gift to support youth education and outreach and inspire curiosity in bright young minds.

Demonstrate your commitment to the natural world and **leave an impression that stands the test of time**.

The award-winning architecture of the Museum's home, the Rio Tinto Center, provides an excellent trailhead to the state's stunning landscapes, diverse lifeforms, and rich cultural history.

Figure 4.4. Natural History Museum of Art campaign promotion. Courtesy of the Natural History Museum of Utah.

CAMPAIGN POLICIES AND PROCEDURES

In addition to the structures to be established for gift administration, I also encourage the preparation of materials and resources specific to a campaign. First, consider if you wish to launch a formal campaign at all. Many organizations welcome endowment gifts without ever formally commencing an endowment campaign and rely on committed donors and trustees to fund the endowment, which is perfectly acceptable. If you do make the decision to present a formal endowment campaign to the community, here are some elements of the campaign to prepare:

- *Establishment of board expectations.* Most important and before all else, it is absolutely essential that the board members that govern the museum are supportive of an endowment campaign. Board members' contributions often form the nucleus of financial support for any campaign, and their support in the community can provide additional momentum. From financial contributions to service to community relations, this can be a time for your trustees to shine.
- *Determination of campaign goal.* As with all campaigns, setting a dollar amount to reach is a collective goal that can be publicized. Momentum can be built toward this goal. The number should be more than you think you need—always the case!—and for an endowment campaign, determined by the annual distribution amount that will positively impact either the entirety of the operating budget, or specific programs or staff positions.
- *Development of case statement.* Following internal discussions and external communication with potential stakeholders, a case statement is developed that provides a justification for the campaign, details campaign goals and potential outcomes, and builds support for the campaign. I include in figure 4.4 a sample page from a case statement from the Natural History Museum of Utah for reference.
- *Creation of campaign timeline.* A campaign timeline should consider both internal needs and development department goals, as well as external needs. What is a realistic timeline for completion given the current staff size and board competencies? Are there campaigns expected to take place in the community that may influence how tight or extensive a campaign timeline is? Keep in mind that a campaign is active when a board of trustees votes to begin it, and concludes when the goal is met. Gifts can and should be directed to endowment funds after a formal campaign has concluded, but a timeline should be one that is reasonably accommodated by the staff and palatable to the community. A two- or three-year campaign is typical to reach a milestone; a campaign that lasts a decade begs inquiry into institutional goal-setting and will almost certainly lose momentum.
- *Structure of solicitation methods.* Your solicitation sequence will most likely consist of a combination of communication methods, ranging from mailings to social media and emails to offer general promotion of the campaign to the com-

munity, alongside targeted engagement with donors via phone and in-person visits. Trustees can be valuable allies in planning for donor engagement, which can consist of social gatherings with museum leadership. Consider the costs, time commitment, and materials to support the different forms of engagement.

- *Communication with fund managers.* As discussed previously, institutions should have established relationships with fund managers, either via community foundations or other third-party organizations, or directly with investment firms. While it is best practices to maintain consistent relationships with these contacts, it is particularly important to do so when anticipating a campaign and soliciting funds to be invested and to prepare fund managers accordingly.
- *Establishment of staff expectations.* As we know, most museums could always do with more staff. Invaluable to a successful campaign is the awareness of staff capacity and the ability to manage a campaign effectively. This can be accomplished through strong staff leadership and support from trustees and volunteers; if possible, additional staff can be brought on during an active campaign to oversee processing and donor communications.

The above considerations should provide a template for the creation of the fundamental resources for beginning a campaign, though that is certainly not where expectations end. The time during and after an active campaign is just as

Figure 4.5. The Goodwin Mansion at Strawbery Banke. Courtesy of David J. Murray / ClearEyePhoto.com.

relevant, and the organization should be equipped to receive gifts at any time and in any form. Individual gifts made of cash or cash equivalents, planned giving, and pledges will all take shape, and the staff and board should be able to accommodate them all.

Remember the discussion about campaign timelines? While you don't want a formal campaign to exist indefinitely, you certainly want to maintain interest in the endowment far into the future and past the formal campaign phase. Your organization should offer endowment funding as a perennial fundraising option, available to donors as part of the permanent endowment program. Some organizations may choose to restrict a portion of the annual fund campaign to the endowment in a given year, or to regularly request endowment support from the board, either from new members or according a schedule every few years. In any case, paramount in all of these arrangements is the value of communication, transparency, and mutual understanding. It is vital to continuously express gratitude and the importance of a shared vision of the future.

* * * * *

CASE STUDY: STRAWBERY BANKE MUSEUM
PORTSMOUTH, NEW HAMPSHIRE

Mission: To promote understanding of the lives of individuals and the value of a community through encounters with the history and ongoing preservation of a New England waterfront neighborhood.

A ten-acre outdoor history museum located in downtown Portsmouth, New Hampshire, Strawbery Banke Museum was originally the grounds of the Abenaki tribe and later colonized by the British sea captain Walter Neale. Named for the berries that grow along the Piscataqua River, the site existed as a residential neighborhood for over three centuries. In the mid-1950s, the historic buildings of the area were considered for potential demolition, and ultimately rescued by a group of preservationists, which formed the basis for Strawbery Banke. It opened as a museum in 1965, and was instrumental in the 1966 National Preservation Act as the first site to receive federal funds via the urban renewal program to support historic preservation rather than structural demolition.[2]

Today, Strawbery Banke is a cultural destination that welcomes more than 110,000 visitors every year and consists of forty historic structures, exhibition spaces, outdoor gardens, and a seasonal ice-skating rink. Craftspeople, artisans, and costumed role-players engage visitors. Drawing on its founding principles, Strawbery Banke continues to prize community support and participation, which is evident in its leadership and current funding structures.

Strawbery Banke maintains an annual budget of just over $3 million and employs between 100 and 120 individuals in a typical year. The operation is supported with an extensive fundraising program, which includes: the 1630 Society for those who contribute $1,000 or more per year; the Puddle Dock Society, established as a planned giving program by trustees in 1998; an annual giving program; and corporate sponsorships.

In terms of its endowments, Strawbery Banke maintains a number of restricted and unrestricted funds, some of which are held and managed directly by Strawbery Banke, others overseen by outside firms: one is an investment of which Strawbery Banke is one of a number of benefactors, and the spending determined by the managers of the fund; another, consisting of donor-directed funds managed via a charitable trust. The unrestricted endowment of Strawbery Banke currently totals $4.4 million, with an additional $3 million pledged as part of a coordinated growth strategy. Additional funds are restricted to a building restoration fund, care of the historic gardens, and the Shapiro House Fund, which is restricted to the maintenance of a particular structure on the Strawbery Banke site and funded primarily by the descendants of the Shapiro family, a former resident. Immediate needs are accommodated by a separate reserve fund that totals approximately $350,000 that is set aside for additional and/or urgent needs.

Larry Yerdon, the president and CEO of Strawbery Banke, arrived in 2004 and concurrent with a complete overhaul of the investments instigated by Strawbery Banke's investment committee. The committee shifted from passive to active fund management and today prioritizes fund growth. Specifically, Yerdon and the committee are keen to secure funding for former residences following the model of the Shapiro House, in which family members are invited to act as stewards of their ancestors' family homes. While Yerdon generally prefers unrestricted funds versus those with restrictions, he explains that the possibility to fund the specific structures via their own support streams establishes future sustainability and a sense of permanence.[3]

Strawbery Banke is in the midst of a $25 million campaign that includes fundraising for the endowment. As of 2021, the campaign has already raised $20 million via cash donations, planned giving, and pledges. The campaign resources encourage donors to focus on planned giving and general endowment support to be designated by the organization as needed. As Yerdon explains, the concentration of donor messaging on planned giving is the best use of the staff capacities and skills in the development department, and encourages donors to participate in planning the future of the institution. The case statement details the need to support endowments, and specific initiatives include the amount needed to underwrite an endowment gift to support each area of focus. (See figures 4.6–4.8.)

The 2020 COVID-19 pandemic has played a role, with original timelines and prospective donor lists discarded as the pandemic continued throughout 2020 and 2021, and campaign planning materials revised accordingly. While potential lead donors were not necessarily negatively impacted by the pandemic in terms of their financial position, the inability to meet donors in person was a major hurdle to the campaign progressing as originally planned. Though donor engagement necessarily

THROUGH OUR **ENDOWMENT**, WE KEEP AN EYE ON THE FUTURE AS WE STEWARD THE PAST.

Currently, Strawbery Banke's invested monies stand at $9 million—which is not in line with its caliber, size or scope of programming. The majority of our peer museums have endowments that are significantly larger.

We must increase our endowment to elevate Strawbery Banke at all levels— positioning the Museum for extraordinary success well into the future. The principal of any endowed funds will remain invested in perpetuity, while generated income will be directed toward designated purposes.

▪ Using the New England Museum Association's Salary Survey as a gauge, salaries at Strawbery Banke fall well below the average. We must offer more competitive salaries to attract and retain the most talented staff.

▪ Twenty percent of the ten thousand schoolchildren we serve each year come from under-resourced districts. By growing our *History Within Reach* scholarship program, we will double the number of economically disadvantaged children we impact.

▪ While the Heritage House Program, admission fees, and facility rental income contribute significantly to our bottom line, additional support from a more robust endowment is essential to operating a world-class museum.

Figure 4.6. Strawbery Banke campaign brochure sample. Courtesy of Strawbery Banke.

Interpretation & Education Programs

$1.5 million

for program endowment

OUR **INTERPRETATION PROGRAMS** FOCUS ON THE NARRATIVE OF AMERICA.

Using our buildings, landscapes, and collections to set the stage, the Museum's interpretation programs draw visitors into an extraordinarily compelling plot: How does a neighborhood evolve over time in response to economic, social, political, cultural, and climatic changes?

Through the themes of resiliency, adaptability, ingenuity, and community, we invite visitors to consider the commonplace in a new light—by exploring the lives of everyday Americans across cultural, social, and generational boundaries.

By sharing centuries of stories about Puddle Dock residents from all walks of life, we hope to impart one of history's most important lessons: that empathy builds community. In nurturing respect for the multiple perspectives of all, neighborhoods and nations thrive.

- At Penhallow, we will tell the story of an African-American family who resided there in the mid-twentieth century. The Richardsons had strong ties to Portsmouth's Naval Shipyard during World War II and were active in the Civil Rights Movement.

- At the Yeaton-Walsh House, we will interpret the story of the Welch family over multiple generations. After fleeing Ireland's potato famine in 1850, the Welches settled in Portsmouth where they became firmly established in the community.

- In the Captain Walsh House, visitors will step into history as they discover journals in drawers, try on period clothes, and study navigation maps to learn about maritime life in the early 19th century.

- In interpreting nearly four centuries of historic gardens, we use our living collections to teach about change over time in the landscape. We will expand efforts to preserve heirloom plants and gardens, and offer new horticulture programs for the public.

The birth certificates of siblings John and Katy Welch, who lived in the Yeaton-Walsh House (1803).

Figure 4.7. Strawbery Banke campaign brochure sample. Courtesy of Strawbery Banke.

INVESTMENT **OPPORTUNITIES** & WAYS TO GIVE

To achieve the aspirations outlined in this case, Strawbery Banke seeks to raise $13 million for capital, program, and endowment needs over the next five years. There are many ways you can help the Museum achieve its goals:

Restricted & Unrestricted Gifts

Gifts of any size may be designated for a specific campaign goal or made without restrictions. Unrestricted gifts have the advantage of enabling Strawbery Banke to allocate the funds where they are most needed.

Gifts of Cash & Securities

Most gifts to the campaign will be cash contributions. Pledges to the campaign may be paid over a period of up to five years. We also invite gifts of appreciated securities.

Named Gifts

To inspire transformational gifts, Strawbery Banke is offering naming opportunities that allow donors to link their support to specific initiatives and hallmark programs. These naming opportunities are offered both in perpetuity and for terms of years.

Planned Gifts

Strawbery Banke welcomes planned gifts, including trusts, bequests, gifts of fully paid whole life insurance policies, and qualified retirement plan assets. Donors may enjoy full tax benefits for such gifts, while making a lasting contribution to the Museum.

The Annual Fund

Throughout the campaign, Strawbery Banke will continue to solicit gifts for The Annual Fund, the Museum's most dependable, flexible, and impactful source of unrestricted support.

We invite your partnership and support.

Figure 4.8. Strawbery Banke campaign brochure sample. Courtesy of Strawbery Banke.

slowed because of the pandemic, Yerdon comments that the strong performance by Strawbery Banke in response to the pandemic attracted new prospects, and the donor list may look different, but not limited, at this stage in the campaign.

What Can We Learn?

- *The incorporation of endowment funding in a campaign signals organizational strength.* When Yerdon first arrived in 2004, a misassumption existed that Strawbery Banke was in dire financial condition. Through strong management, increased site maintenance, and the public positioning of Strawbery Banke as a community anchor—especially during the pandemic—the perfect climate has been created for potential stakeholders to support its future via the endowment.
- *Adaptability is key.* Endowment growth is an extended investment of time, expertise, and resources. Because Yerdon and his team faced the realities of the pandemic and shifted course as needed, they maintained the support of their donors and even increasing campaign confidence.

* * * * *

ENDOWMENT DONORS: HOW TO FIND THEM

The donor to an endowment fund is not your typical donor. It is not someone who is new to the organization or to philanthropic giving, and most likely not the person who maintains a membership to the institution but is not involved. This is not to say that an endowment gift from such people would not be welcome, but more of a pleasant surprise. Let's talk for a bit about how to determine where to expend energy to solicit endowment gifts with the highest potential efficacy.

The first place from which to gather support is from the board of trustees. As discussed earlier, the board is an essential partner to the staff in determining the vision of the organization and is, of course, responsible for its governance and overall fiscal health. The board of trustees contributes service, expertise, and financial contributions to ensure the longevity and strength of a museum, and therefore should spearhead any endowment campaign.

The support of the board can be solicited in a number of ways. The first is to seek individual gifts from high net worth trustees to lead the pack in terms of giving substantially to a campaign. Another option is to collectivize the financial support of the board in one fund, where the gifts are commingled under a general name and purpose as agreed upon by the board as a whole. This can be a suitable option for boards that consist of members with relatively modest giving capacity. Additionally, and for those trustees that have already structured a planned gift to the institution, a portion can be designated for endowment, which is a popular choice for many as it does not require another contribution.

Trustees are an invaluable link to the community, and may be able to build the donor network of the institution. As we know, fundraising is really about building relationships, and endowment fundraising is particularly successful when long-standing connections between the community and the organization are in place. It is essential that donors feel a bond with the organization, and often those who are most responsive to endowment campaigns are those who have given consistently in the past and understand organizational needs. Donors with extensive philanthropic service are those most understanding of the value of the endowment for the stability a strong endowment offers, and will also hold high expectations for the organization in terms of reporting and compliance.

At the same time, do not underestimate the community members who have a strong bond with the organization, which is where your trustees can serve an important role. Staff members in a development department are most often charged with asking for support for the organization, but especially during campaigns or calculated pushes for support, additional voices can be powerful. Furthermore, the trustees of young or small organization often *are* the fundraisers in the absence of a professional development staff. Encouraging board members to share their reasons for supporting an organization can model behavior to other potential donors, and involving board members in direct asks to their peers can be unbelievably powerful. Consider if there are board members who would be comfortable working with the staff in such a way, or being trained as effective spokespeople and solicitors on behalf of the organization.

Another well to tap is that of the staff itself. When funding endowments, the inclusion in solicitations of staff members whose work will directly benefit from the support can work wonders. The director of the site is highly visible in any fundraising initiative and should be able to speak to the future and vision of an organization, with comprehensive knowledge of institutional planning. Yet fundraising work is not limited to the director and the development team, and other staff members can prove effective as collaborators. Because endowment funding is inextricably linked to the mission of the institution, it is important to invite staff to provide insights into everyday operations and how that mission is brought to life. Curatorial and collections staff (including registrars, archivists, etc.) are experts in the collections of a museum and can illuminate goals for building and stewarding the collection through acquisitions, conservation, or exhibitions funding. Team members in the educational department can offer stories of school visits, educational programs, and the value of providing long-term support to initiatives with an educational benefit. Others, such as visitor services staff, often form relationships with visitors, donors, and trustees, and can offer evidence of the valuable role the organization serves to the community and cite positive feedback from guests. Many members of the staff who typically function far outside the realm of development work can prove to be powerful allies, especially in the context of long-term support for operations and specific areas of need. A donor may be an art collector who is enthusiastic enough to support a new acquisitions fund after only having a conversation with the curator.

Another may talk to an educator about the struggle to keep up with technology and the need to have media that can reach students in classrooms before a field trip, and ultimately create an educational technology fund.

Building personal connections can directly benefit endowments to fund programs, as well as staff positions themselves. Many institutions fund director and curator positions in particular from dedicated endowments. Endowing positions both protects the salary from operational losses and lends prestige to institutions. A 2016 *Inside Philanthropy* article profiles the Saint Louis Art Museum and the Milwaukee Art Museum, institutions where major endowments were established to directly fund the director staff position.[4] According to Brent Benjamin, the former Barbara B. Taylor Director of the Saint Louis Art Museum, endowing the director position "means the museum can compete in the national and international markets for talent."[5] Wisconsin-based philanthropist Donna Baumgartner offers: "We've been so inspired by [the Donald and Donna Baumgartner Director] Dan Keegan's leadership and vision for the future, in particular his passion for securing the viability of the museum for generations to come. We wanted to carry on his legacy and keep the momentum going."[6] Notably, such endowed positions are not necessarily intended to keep individuals in the positions once the funds are established—indeed, both Benjamin and Keegan have since moved on—but to demonstrate a high regard for and protection of the position and its compensation.

All of these recommendations regarding attracting donors to endowment funding speak to the importance of creating mission resonance for donors based

Figure 4.9. Discovery Museum. Courtesy of the Discovery Museum.

on their history with the organization, their kinship with the mission activities, and their ability and willingness to act philanthropically. While there are certainly no guarantees in the world of fundraising, these recommendations may provide some direction as to the best use of staff and trustee time and expertise.[7]

★ ★ ★ ★ ★

CASE STUDY: DISCOVERY MUSEUM
ACTON, MASSACHUSETTS

Mission: To spark delight in learning by igniting curiosity and creativity in children and adults, as they discover together the joys of science, nature, and play.

The Discovery Museum is a relatively young museum, founded in 1982 as the Children's Discovery Museum and originally housed in an 1880 Victorian residence. In 1987, the site expanded to include the Science Discovery Museum, a purpose-built, postmodern structure. The museum continued to flourish there until 2008, when a master plan was conducted following the purchase of an adjacent parcel of land. Discovery Woods soon followed, which includes outdoor activities, installations, and abuts 183 acres of conservation land that is used for programming purposes. A complete renovation and expansion project overhauled the previously disparate buildings and synthesized them into one Americans with Disabilities Act (ADA)-compliant facility, and since then accessibility has remained a major focus of the Discovery Museum visitor experience.

Today, the Discovery Museum site consists of its 2018 building and Discovery Woods, which includes an outdoor nature playscape and tree house. The annual operating budget of the museum is typically between $2.5 and $2.7 million, which supports a staff of approximately thirty-five full-time team members. Director Neil Gordon has been in his position since 2009 and considers it the mission of the institution to promote the STEAM (Science, Technology, Engineering, Art, Math) learning approach.[8] In addition to the 501(c)(3) governing board of directors, additional advisory councils provide expertise and guidance on specific content areas such as math, science, and technology.

The endowment for the Discovery Museum is currently valued at $325,000. Approximately $135,000 of the fund is a permanent endowment that was originally gifted to the Discovery Museum by a collective group of donors. The endowment does not currently support any of the operating costs of the museum and is in a relatively dormant stage according to Gordon. Gifts to the endowment are accepted, but there is no active solicitation for endowment gifts.[9] The endowment is relatively modest in scale and activity, but that does not mean it is not well managed—it is managed by the standing finance committee and subject to an investment policy that is reviewed every two years. The distribution rate is capped at 5 percent of the fund value and according to a rolling three-year average. Additionally, a $1 million reserve fund is available for immediate needs.

As a relatively young museum, Gordon explains that the institutional life cycle of the Discovery Museum plays a major factor in endowment relevance and activity. He notes that when he arrived in 2009, there was less than $8,000 in the bank. Since then, strengthening operating capital has been their central focus. In 2020, the COVID-19 pandemic roiled the museum's financial state, and while Gordon is pleased that there were no losses to staff positions, the annual operating budget was demolished, from $2.8 million to a revised budget of $1.9 million. Following the pandemic, the Discovery Museum is concentrating on rebuilding its operations, financial health, and risk mitigation.

Since Gordon's arrival, the Discovery Museum has focused both time and financial investments on community relations, public engagement, and site upkeep. The attention to the property maintenance has reaped rewards, with returns on property investments such as solar power offsetting operational costs. Gordon explains that their donor base has essentially been built from scratch, and their activity has been based almost completely on meeting current needs. Equipped with a fundraising goal of three and a half times the annual operating budget, the finance committee and board of trustees are laying the groundwork to shift the focus from current operations to the future of the institution. As the Discovery Museum evolves to attend to its future needs, it builds its message of resilience and sustainability.

What Can We Learn?

- *Consider the role of endowments in the life cycle of an institution.* The Discovery Museum is in a passive phase of accepting gifts to the endowment following rigorous fundraising in its earliest stages, but is in a period of growth and response to current needs.
- *The ability to actively solicit endowment gifts is indicative of the current state of an organization, though by no means is an organization unsuccessful if it is still in the preparatory phase.* At the Discovery Museum, the organization is building its donor base and its operational confidence, necessities for all museums but particularly children's museums, which often suffer from a lack of sustained engagement as their core audiences age. Such planning will benefit endowment building in the long run.

★ ★ ★ ★ ★

ISSUES IN THE FIELD:
POPULAR ASSUMPTIONS ABOUT ENDOWMENTS

The endowment, as we know, is a common topic about museums in the popular press. The stories that run are often about large institutions with high-value endowments, and in the context of controversial practices like "raiding" an endowment, discussed in chapter 3. Larger institutions are certainly not immune to discussions of endowment invasion, and perhaps are more susceptible to criticism of endowment management due to the high values of investments. Charles Venable, formerly the director of Newfields in Indianapolis (formerly known as the Indianapolis Museum of Art), made the controversial decision to eliminate free admission and modify endowment usage to whittle away long-standing debts. The Newfields endowment is one of the largest in the country—at a hefty $335 million—but it has only realized growth of 3 percent over the past decade. For reference, the Standard & Poor's 500 Index (S&P) has grown more than 15 percent in the same time period.[10] Meanwhile, the debt has persisted at virtually the same amount since 2011, in the mid-$300 millions.[11] Other institutions, such as the Metropolitan Museum of Art, host massive endowments that are indispensable to operations, but which are heavily invested and less accessible. The Met's endowment, for example, is $3.6 billion, more than ten times its annual operating budget.[12] In times of economic distress, organizations such as Newfields and the Met can face public outcry over the fact that they have investments at such high values.

These organizations with expansive asset bases are an atypical segment of the museum population. While they receive the most national coverage, they are not representative of the many small, midsized, and relatively large institutions that maintain endowments and other investments that are more scalable. The popular press can, whether intentional or not, court suspicion that nonprofit organizations are begging for money while hording millions in their coffers, which is by and large not the case. Furthermore, this is not a new topic: one needs only to look at two *New York Times* pieces from 1988, "Museum's Downfall: Raiding Endowment to Pay for Growth" and "Historical Society Cuts Staff in Budget Crisis," both about the New-York Historical Society, to see that pieces critical of endowment use, particularly during times of emergency, have persisted for decades.[13] While actions such as raiding endowments and sales of works in a permanent collection are verboten in the museum field, we should remember that national coverage of such topics certainly breeds concern among donors. Donor communications and maintaining compliant procedures can encourage strong messaging to potential donors, and build the optimism and confidence necessary for donor relations to flourish.

* * * * *

CONCLUSION

The endowment is an incomparable means of support for an organization. At the same time, fundraising for endowments can prove challenging, often because it requires investment in an organization's future and often without immediate results. For the right donors, and at the right time in the institution's life cycle, the endowment can prove to be a fruitful form of support for its regenerative nature and its indefatigable role in financial sustainability.

Key Points: What Have We Learned?

- Endowments are all about timing, both in terms of the institutional evolution and in the context of the markets, the economy, and public perception of the cultural sector. Simply look at how COVID-19 impacted the activities of the case studies in this chapter to see how two organizations navigated unexpected needs and endowment expectations.
- Raising funds, for endowments and for all else, is a team sport. Planning and execution should involve team members from the board, the staff, and from departments not necessarily affiliated with fundraising for maximum impact. When multiple voices extol the virtues of an organization and the possibilities for its future, the donor response can be extraordinarily positive.

NOTES

1. Lynda S. Moerschenbaecher, *Building an Endowment Right from the Start* (Chicago: Precept Press, 2001), 8.
2. "Strawbery Banke Museum Mission, History, and Vision Statement," Strawbery Banke Museum website, https://www.strawberybanke.org/people/mission-history .cfm.
3. Larry Yerdon, interview with Rebekah Beaulieu, May 14, 2021.
4. Mike Scutari, "A Quick Look at Another Big Give to Endow a Museum Directorship," *Inside Philanthropy*, May 31, 2016, https://www.insidephilanthropy.com/home/2016/ 5/31/a-quick-look-at-another-big-give-to-endow-a-museum-directors .html.
5. Scutari, "A Quick Look at Another Big Give to Endow a Museum Directorship."
6. Ibid.
7. These recommendations support the LIA fundraising model. L: linkage to institution; I: interest in mission; A: ability to give. See https://summitfundraising.co.uk/priori tise-how-to-use-the-l-i-a-model/ for more information.
8. Neil Gordon, interview with Rebekah Beaulieu, March 29, 2021.
9. Ibid.
10. Maxwell Anderson, "I Led the Indianapolis Museum of Art for Five Years. Here's How Charles Venable, Its Recently Ousted President, Failed the Institution," *ArtNet*, February 23, 2021, https://news.artnet.com/opinion/indianapolis-muse um-of-art-maxwell-anderson-1945878.
11. Andrew Russeth, "The Ringmaster: Is Charles Venable Democratizing and Great Art Museum in Indianapolis—or Destroying It?" *Art News*, July 9, 2019, https:// www.artnews.com/art-news/news/charles-venable-newfields-indianapolis-mu seum-12938/.
12. Valentina Di Liscia, "Why Art Museums Can't Always Fall Back on Endowments," *Hyperallergic*, April 15, 2020. https://hyperallergic.com/556133/why-museums -cant-always-fall-back-on-endowments/.

13. Douglas C. McGill, "Museum's Downfall: Raiding Endowment to Pay for Growth," *New York Times*, July 19, 1988, https://www.nytimes.com/1988/07/19/arts/muse um-s-downfall-raiding-endowment-to-pay-for-growth.html; Douglass C. McGill, "Historical Society Cuts Staff in Budget Crisis," *New York Times*, June 30, 1988, https://www.nytimes.com/1988/06/30/arts/historical-society-cuts-staff-in-bud get-crisis.html.

5

The Public Face

THE ENDOWMENT AND FINANCIAL TRANSPARENCY

When we reflect on the value of understanding endowments and their function in the financial support structure of an institution, we tend to focus inward. The donor relationships that fund endowments are highly individualized and relate to institutional priorities; yet the management of the funds themselves is often embedded in general financial management and in relationships with outside investment managers. Yet, as will be seen in this chapter, the management of endowments themselves is a topic of increasing public interest, seen as a barometer of an organization's true commitment to its future, its ideals, and its relationship to social justice. This chapter introduces the concept of financial transparency and the relationship of endowment management to mission relevance.

WHAT IS FINANCIAL TRANSPARENCY?

Financial transparency is required of all tax-exempt organizations in the United States as a means to provide clarity into how money is managed, particularly money received via tax-deductible contributions from federal and private sources. Transparency is the organization's ability and willingness to disclose financial information in a timely and compliant manner.

The IRS Form 990

The most basic methods for financial disclosures are comprised in the annual reporting structure, which consists of the annual tax filing and, for those organizations for which it is required, the annual audit. Form 990 is the return of organization(s) exempt from income tax, and takes many forms depending on the organizational size and incorporation structure. For those that are incorporated as foundations, for instance, the 990-PF is particular to foundation structures. Museums that function as part of larger incorporated entities, like the Colonial Dames of America or the Daughters of the American Revolution membership organizations, may not file their own 990s. Every organization granted a tax exemption is required by law to disclose the financial activities on an annual basis. The financial activity is filed with the government, portions of which are made available to the general public.[1]

The Annual Audit Process

In addition to the 990, most organizations are responsible for the completion of an annual audit. The audit is an independent examination of an organization's financial systems and procedures. The audit process is typically completed on an annual basis and conducted by an external financial services firm to ensure objectivity. Auditors review internal documents and records of financial activity over the period of review, resulting in the opinion letter and financial statement and notes. The financial statements are comprised of the following:

- *Statement of financial position.* A comprehensive record of organizational financial standing, which is also known as the balance sheet.
- *Statement of financial activity.* The document showing the income and expenditures of an organization and how they relate to each other. This is also known as the income statement of profit and loss (P&L) statement.
- *Statement of cash flows.* The accounting of the change in cash and cash equivalents during a financial period, summarizing the sources and uses of cash during that time. The statement of cash flows is not required as part of the audit in all states.
- *Statement of functional expenses.* The documentation of organizational expenses by functional area, typically designated into programming and administrative categorizations.

The role of the auditors is not to provide substantive feedback regarding the health of the organization but to certify that financial management procedures are in place. The opinion letter will state whether or not the organization is fairly presenting its financial statements and is compliant with generally accepted accounting principles (GAAP). This letter is a critical record of organizational health and transparency, often included along with the financial statements in applications for grants and sponsorships.

Financial Statements and Endowment Reporting

Just as endowments are unique in their daily management and operational use, they require special consideration in terms of the annual financial reporting process. Endowments are typically recorded in the statement of financial position as an asset or group of assets, depending on the number and type of investments the organization holds. The documentation of funds has shifted since 2017, when the Financial Accounting Standards Board (FASB) no longer required nonprofit organizations to delineate between temporarily restricted and permanently restricted funds. Today, FASB requires only a separation of unrestricted and restricted funds. What does that mean? Post-2017 financial statements articulate unrestricted funds, those not beholden by any restrictions and available for any use as approved by the organization's governing body, and restricted funds, which include both those that are temporarily restricted (to be used for a specific purpose and/or within a specific timeframe, often internally designated) and those that are permanently restricted (funds to be used only according to the wishes of the donor and of which the principal is to remain untouched). According to these rules, endowments are documented as a restricted fund, and starting and ending balances available as part of the disclosure process. The notes to the financial statements often provide additional information to contextualize the numerical data, such as the spending rate and any changes to investment policies or fund restrictions.

The Annual Report and Transparency

Conventionally, the completion of the organization's financial statements and 990 filing would complete the annual financial report. And in the past, that would be enough; if someone wished to view these documents, they could request them of the organization itself or via the state office of the attorney general. Today, however, expectations regarding financial transparency have heightened. Many organizations now publish annual reports that include the entirety of the financial statements or a summary of major information, investment balances that highlight any endowment activity over the reporting period, and other, nonfinancial information, such as data on visitation and audience development, programming, outreach, and other mission-relevant activities. The annual report has evolved from a financial checklist completed for legal purposes to a public-facing chronicle of organizational activities, designed to engage potential members and donors.

This transformation of the annual report helps us to understand the shifting role of financial transparency and its growing importance in the public arena. No longer just a record of legal compliance, the annual report and its associated financial data is used for donor cultivation and solicitation, and general public engagement, and it is provided in grants and stewardship reports along with audited financial statements to evidence organizational health and mission focus. Many organizations now provide access to financial statements, 990 filings, and annual reports on their own websites, or upload such information to charitynavigator. org or guidestar.org, both of which serve as clearinghouse sites for nonprofit data. Recognizing that nonprofit financial records are available via such platforms, many organizations have embraced transparency, both to assure accuracy of the information disseminated online and to strengthen institutional identity.

The relevance of financial transparency to institutional relevance and mission is a relatively new concept, asserted in both the wide availability of data, as well as changing guidelines that now require organizations to detail their financial investments in mission work via the statement of functional expenses. Many organizations looking to present themselves as healthy and mission focused see the value of the creation of an institutional narrative that marries mission relevance, institutional planning, and financial compliance. This can also help the public understand fluctuations in financial activity: a museum that is in the process of acquiring land or building an expansion may have financial records that show a large amount of cash and cash equivalents in one year, and low liquidity in the year the project has been completed and the bills paid. A comprehensive annual report, if available, can help the public understand the seeming volatility as a healthy move toward institutional growth. The more an organization can foster understanding of and commitment to its future via financial reporting systems, the better the likelihood of community support.

* * * * *

CASE STUDY: MARYHILL MUSEUM OF ART
GOLDENDALE, WASHINGTON

Mission: From the unique Columbia River Gorge, Maryhill Museum of Art collects, presents, and preserves art and historical and natural resources to enrich and educate residence and visitors of the Pacific Northwest.

When Samuel Hill relocated from Minnesota to Washington in 1907, he arrived with the intention to build a Quaker farming community. Instead, he became the president of the Seattle Gas and Electric Company and is widely considered to be a fundamental player in the industrialization of the Pacific Northwest. Following a rapid ascent, Hill began construction on a new home in 1914, situated on 26 acres and designed by Hornblower & Marshall, a renowned architectural firm based out of Washington, DC. The remote location and lack of irrigation ultimately prevented the use of the site as a residence, and so Hill revised his plans and decided to complete the building for use as a museum. The building was completed in 1926 and within its walls were exhibited objects from Hill's personal art collection, including more than seventy sculptures and watercolors by Auguste Rodin, as well as additions to the collection contributed by others such as Queen Marie of Romania, who gave Russian folk objects, icons, and textiles. The building itself was an icon of early-twentieth-century design, its Beaux-Arts façade supported by a completely steel structure.

Figure 5.1. Maryhill Museum of Art. Courtesy of the Maryhill Museum of Art.

Following Hill's death in 1931 and a protracted legal process, the site was finally open to the public in 1940. Today, the museum sits on a sprawling 5,300-acre site adjacent to the Columbia River Gorge. In addition to its original 1926 building, the museum includes the Bruce and Mary Stevenson Wing, which opened in 2012 and consists of an education center, a contemporary art exhibition space, collections storage, and a café. Additional outdoor spaces populate and interpret the landscape of the museum, which maintains a seasonal schedule and is open from March through November.

The museum functions on an annual budget of approximately $1.2 million, which supports a staff of eight full-time and six seasonal staff members.[2] Director Colleen Schafroth has been with the organization since the 1980s, and was appointed director of the Maryhill Museum in 2001. During her tenure, the museum has diversified its income, which includes earnings from ranching leases, and focused on sustainability, such as the installation of wind turbines on the grounds.

Endowment income is a small yet steady source of operational support, and the endowment will be a focus of institutional growth in the coming years. The endowment portfolio of the museum consists of a variety of funds, including the Maryhill Endowment, which supports operating needs; the Gammel Fund, which is restricted to the conservation and care of "The Hounds" series of paintings by American artist R. H. Ives Gammel and curatorial staff salaries; and the Sam Hill Reserve Fund, which dates to the 1930s and was established with a gift of treasury bonds.

In 2021, the total endowment was $2 million, and spending is based on a three-year portfolio valuation average and not to exceed 5 percent of this calculation. The investments are overseen by the finance committee, who reviews and updates the investment policy on an annual basis. Schafroth and the finance committee have exercised prudent oversight of the endowment; their goal is to keep the principal intact and maintain stability. This approach has been well received, with the Bruce and Mary Stevenson Foundation supporting endowment growth via an annual $100,000 restricted to endowment principal. Schafroth explains that she would like to grow the endowment to $5 million and regularly communicates with the board of trustees regarding the strategy to utilize only the annual distribution of the endowment to ensure strength of the principal.[3]

According to Schafroth, transparency is a top priority at the museum. It has been an active initiative rather than a rote annual necessity. The Maryhill Museum website includes core documents of the museum, such as its bylaws, articles of incorporation, investment policy, endowment and reserve policy, code of ethics, and whistleblower policy (see figure 5.2). The museum has benefitted from the transparent actions, which has won appreciation from donors as to the museum's willingness to share information widely and without request, and confidence from potential stakeholders and the general community.

What Can We Learn?

- *Slow and steady wins the race.* Through strict use policies, consistent board education, and strong relationships, the Maryhill Museum of Art is able to grow its endowment on a small budget and with consistent attention to full transparency.
- *Financial stability is a benefit of diversified income streams.* The ability to make modest use of the endowment in the operating needs of the museum is made possible by income generated via land leasing agreements, along with reserve and cost-saving measures.

INVESTMENTS AND MISSION RELEVANCE

In recent years, conversations regarding investment methodologies have extended beyond concerns solely related to institutional health. While the actual investment of institutional funds is certainly best left to the experts licensed to do so, many nonprofit organizations have elected to actively review the companies and industries in which endowment funds are invested, looking beyond financial performance to substantive issues of mission relevance. In this case, mission relevance may be considered in terms of ethical compatibility as it relates to environmental and social issues, governance structures, and equity.

The first organizations to address mission relevance were faith-based, and the first widely documented instance of such activity was the 2003 passage of the socially

MARYHILL
MUSEUM
ᴸᴸ₀ART

Endowment, Reserves and Funds Policy

PURPOSE
The purpose of this policy for Maryhill Museum of Art is to ensure the stability of the mission, programs, employment, and ongoing operations of the organization. Maryhill Museum of Art has one endowment, and three other funds They are:

1. **The Maryhill Endowment:** Established in 2003, this endowment is the museum's main operating endowment. The Board of Trustees combined the Nicholas and Antoinette Comnene Endowment Fund (begun by Irene Bie in 1987 with a gift of $100,000 and completed with $100,000 out of her bequest of 2001) and the Stevenson Endowment Fund (started by the Mary Hoyt Stevenson Foundation) to create the Maryhill Endowment (Minutes: January 18, 2003). Gifts to the Maryhill Endowment are permanently restricted gifts.

2. **The Gammell Fund:** Established in 2000 with a gift of $160,000 by the R.H. Ives Gammell Trust, this endowment is to be kept as a "separate fund exclusively for the exhibition of *The Hound* (a painting series), to its maintenance, restoration (conservation), insurance against loss, and to the education of the public concerning *The Hound* and the work and artistic influence of R.H. Ives Gammell." The museum is to use its best efforts to "manage the fund as to cause both the capital value of the fund and the amounts expended from it to increase from year to year..." At the time of the gift, $25,000 was authorized by R.H. Ives Gammell Trust by their curator Liz Hunter (Minutes: October 27, 2000) to upgrade collections storage for the care of the paintings. The remaining $135,000 in the Gammell Fund is temporarily restricted. The museum uses this fund to support collections and curatorial staff salaries and annual collections costs as these expenditures are consistent with the wishes of R.H. Ives Gammell Trust as outlined above.

3. **Sam Hill Reserve:** Established when founder Sam Hill's estate was settled in the late 1930s, this reserve is used as an operating reserve but also provides an internal source of funds for situations such as a sudden increase in expenses, one-time unbudgeted expenses, unanticipated loss in funding, or uninsured losses. The fund is a board designated fund. Reserves may also be used for one-time nonrecurring expenses that

Figure 5.2. Maryhill Museum of Art endowment, reserves, and fund policy. Courtesy of the Maryhill Museum of Art.

USE
1. Identification of appropriate use of funds: The Executive Director will identify the need for access to funds and confirm that the use is consistent with the purpose of the endowments or reserves as described in this Policy.
2. Authority to use funds: The Executive Director will submit a request to use to the Board of Trustees. This may be through the annual budgeting process or through a specific request. The request will include the analysis and determination of the use of funds and plans for replenishment (if any).
3. Reporting and monitoring: The Board of Trustees and the Executive Director are responsible for assuring that all funds are maintained and used only as described in this Policy.

RELATIONSHIP TO OTHER POLICIES
Maryhill Museum of Art shall maintain the following board approved policies, which may contain provisions that affect the creation, sufficiency, and management of these funds.

1. Disaster Preparedness Emergency Response Plan
2. Investment Policy
3. Collections Management Policy
4. Fundraising, Gifts and Membership Policy

REVIEW OF POLICY
This Endowment, Reserve and Fund Policy will be reviewed every other year, by the Finance Committee, or sooner if warranted by internal or external events or changes. Changes to the Policy will be recommended by the Finance Committee to the Board of Trustees.

ADOPTION
This statement of Endowment, Reserve and Fund Policy was revised on by the Finance Committee of the Maryhill Museum of Art during its meeting March 30, 2019. This policy supersedes the previous policy adopted by the Board of Trustees November 19, 2011.

Figure 5.2. (*Continued*)

responsible investment guidelines by the United States Conference of Catholic Bishops (USCCB), colloquially known as the Bishops' Guidelines.[4] Antidiscriminatory practices, environmental protections, economic justice, and the protection of human life are all intrinsic to the ideology of the USCCB. The Bishops' Guidelines detail that investments are to be made with firms and in entities that are like-minded, with the intention to serve both "religious mandate and financial responsibility."[5]

Investments dedicated to environmental, social, and governance responsibilities—ESG investments—have received widespread attention. The confluence of financial and ethical responsibilities is now a focus of nonprofit organizations looking to center mission and community development in investing activities. ESG investments comprise a variety of interests such as a dedication to equity, diversity, inclusion, accessibility, or social justice. Equally of interest to those in ESG investing are how a company addresses, represents, and serves its staff, community, and environment. Such qualities are evaluated in terms of the companies in which investments may be made, but also the firms who manage the investments themselves, such as those that are female- or minority-owned.

University endowments have undergone a fundamental shift toward ESG investments. Student involvement and protests against investments in fossil fuels instigated much of the change. By 2021, more than 1,300 educational institutions have divested $14.6 *trillion* from the fossil fuel industry.[6] ESG language is now standard in university investment policies, with Brown University, Harvard University, Boston University, George Washington University, and Columbia University all investing in ESG interests and even hosting courses on the topic.

The increasing—and dare I say, long overdue—scrutiny regarding nonprofit investing activities is only now impacting museums as an activity that can support social and culturally responsible behavior. According to the GoFossilFree.org website, 35 percent of the organizations who have pledged divestment from fossil fuels are faith based, 15 percent are educational institutions, and 14 percent are philanthropic foundations. While only one indicator of ESG investing, it is notable that as of 2021, the percentage of cultural organizations who practice or pledge fossil fuel divestment is so minimal it amounts to 0 percent.[7] While the number of cultural organizations who have yet to commit to divestments—or to general ESG investing priorities—is small, the tide is turning, especially as educational and philanthropic foundation nonprofit organizations receive notice for their activities.

The alignment of organizational mission with firms and corporations, also known as mission-relevant investments (MRI), that reflect institutional values is of increasing priority to museums, not least of all because major funders are taking a lead role. In 2017, the Ford Foundation pledged to reallocate $1 billion of its endowment to ESG interests.[8] In its press release accompanying the announcement, the Ford Foundation noted:

> Our current global capitalist system is increasing inequality. Through Mission Investments, we invest the foundation's capital to help solve some of the

world's greatest social problems through grants, program-related investments (PRI) and mission-related investments (MRI). We aim to influence and mobilize a wide spectrum of capital providers—from institutional investors to banks to retail investors—to develop a more inclusive form of capitalism and create a more economically just world.[9]

Since the Ford Foundation announcement, whether by influence or contemporaneity, a number of arts institutions have incorporated MRI priorities into their fund management. The Field Museum in Chicago and the American Museum of Natural History in New York have divested from fossil fuels and the Massachusetts Museum of Contemporary Art (Mass MOCA) in North Adams, Massachusetts, has shifted its endowment to an ESG strategy. The Phipps Conservatory and Botanical Gardens in Pittsburgh has pledged to support environmental sustainability via its endowment investments. And in international news, the Louvre in Paris has allocated 5 percent of its endowment to socially responsible investments, including artisan crafts, cultural tourism, and heritage interests.[10] Just as museums are being held accountable for the funds they accept from corporations—organizations such as the Metropolitan Museum of Art and the Museum of Modern Art have been criticized for accepting donations from individuals associated with controversial industries such as private prisons, tobacco, and firearms—so are they responsible for where and how their endowments are invested.[11]

Implementation of Mission Relevant Investing

For many of us, the implementation of MRI may seem daunting. You may have inherited an investment policy that has not undergone revision in ages, or you may only be establishing proper policies for the first time. For those who are creating an investment policy from scratch, MRI language can be incorporated into the draft policy and reviewed by the investment committee and approved by the governing board. If an investment policy is in place, it should be reviewed with fund managers to determine the current investing strategy.

In a 2019 blog post for the American Alliance of Museums, Anna Raginskaya of Morgan Stanley offered direction on how to consider and incorporate MRI/ESG interests.[12] Her recommendations include taking the following steps:

- *Restriction screening*—intentionally avoiding certain companies, industries, or countries due to values or risk-based criteria.
  Example: removing exposure to gun manufacturers and distributors in the portfolio.
- *ESG integration*—proactively considering environmental, social, and governance (ESG) criteria alongside financial analysis to identify opportunities and risks during the investment process.

Example: investing in an equity strategy actively tilted toward companies with meaningful practices around board, executive, management, and employee diversity.

- *Thematic exposure*—investing in themes related to solving sustainability related to domestic and global challenges.
  Example: targeted investments in public companies focused on renewable energy.
- *Impact investing*—investing in generally private opportunities that provide capital to businesses focused on creating targeted change through their business model, products, and services.
  Example: a private investment in an agriculture fund that focuses on natural and antibiotic-free crops, quality employment for farm workers, and technological enhancements to drive higher yield and lower land and water use.[13]

Raginskaya's recommendations encourage us to reflect on some of the methodologies for MRI/ESG investments, such as those that practice diversity in staff leadership, thematic focus, and those that support growing business models or services. Such considerations require extensive conversation within the investment and/or finance committees of your governing board, and even the entirety of the board itself. Again quoting Raginskaya, here are some questions to guide your discussion:

- What social and/or environmental challenges does my organization currently help address? Could some of these also be addressed through investments?
- Does it make sense for our organization to develop a mission-aligned investment policy statement?
- Is my current investment advisor equipped to help me learn more about the different approaches to sustainable investing?[14]

The transition to MRI is one that also welcomes dialogue with fund managers, more so than is typically seen in the relationship between most managers and institutions. Many museums practice passive investing, in which the goal is to realize returns with the intent to maintain investments for a duration, often via investing in diversified index funds. Active investing, on the other hand, is more hands-on and asserts active buying and trading of individual investments. Active investing is not as common for long-term nonprofit endowment management; it is less popular because of the need for strong oversight and increased management fees. However, for those interested in encouraging MRI priorities, an organization may enter a period of more active investing to transition to an MRI composition. As MRI fund priorities gain traction in the nonprofit world, there are firms that specialize in such funding models and can work with organizations to assure mission alignment.

In addition to the funds that are directly held by the organizations and managed under their direction, we see many investments held in community foundations or other third parties, with the income transferred to the organization according to donor intent. For those funds that generate income for a museum but are not under its direct management, consult with the foundations themselves regarding MRI focus; while the funds are not under museum direction, it is still important to understand where the investments are held.

Once you have reviewed your investments, you may learn that the organization has indeed invested in funds that are at conflict with the organizational mission. What if you discover that your investments are held in companies with which there is an ethical dilemma? The release or reduction of assets due to financial or ethical reasons is officially known as divestment or divestiture. We commonly hear the term in relation to fossil fuels or hazardous materials, but it is applicable to any reduction in assets. Language regarding divestment procedures should also be incorporated into an updated investment policy.

You may wonder where to look for guidance regarding revision of your investment policy, and this is where our peers in higher education have laid some groundwork. The Intentional Endowments Network, a subset of the Crane Institute of Sustainability, offers a number of references for review. The London School of Economics, for example, has an extensive investment policy that provides comprehensive language. Here is an excerpt:

> The School has a legal obligation and fiduciary responsibility to maximize our charitable income and returns in order to further the School's objectives consistent with our agreed risk appetite established by Council.
>
> The School has adopted the six UN Principles for Responsible Investing, recognising that doing so is an effort to better align it as an investor with broader objectives of society, consistent with the LSE Council's statutory fiduciary responsibilities as charity trustees.
>
> A key aspect of the School's approach to responsible investing is for the Finance Committee and Investment Subcommittee to make investment decisions which take into account environmental, social and corporate governance (ESG) issues in managing the endowment funds in accordance with the UN six Principles and LSE's ethical standards.
>
> The School will not make direct or, as far as possible, indirect investments in equities or bonds issued by companies engaged in tobacco manufacture, indiscriminate arms manufacture or companies which are significantly engaged in the extraction of thermal coal and tar sands, the most polluting of fossil fuels.
>
> The School will, where possible, aim to switch its passively managed equity investments into funds which track indices which more closely meet its SRI objectives, such as the FTSE4Good UK or Global Indices.
>
> The School will seek to progressively reduce its investment in funds which indirectly place its endowment in companies significantly engaged in the extraction of thermal coal and tar sands.
>
> The School will take a pro-active approach in collaborating with other likeminded investors to encourage asset managers to develop new socially responsible investment products.

The Investment Subcommittee, Finance Committee and Council will continue to monitor on-going opportunities to improve socially responsible investing as new opportunities become available.

The School will not invest in "black box" investment vehicles where it is not possible to identify the nature of underlying assets.[15]

The policy of the London School of Economics addresses many of the topics already introduced in this chapter: ESG issues, passive versus active investing strategies, and alignment with fund investors. It even articulates that the school will not invest in any funds for which the nature of the assets is not readily available. Not all institutions require such an extensive catalog of guidelines, or may wish to start on a smaller scale. The Loyola University of Chicago statement is composed of one clause in the policy:

Consistent with achieving the applicable investment objectives set forth herein, the University's investment policy will be implemented within a framework predicated on incorporating environmental, social and governance factors as core components of decision-making and risk management, impact and solutions-based investments, engagement, proxy voting, and evaluation of the economic merits of current and potential investments taking into account governance practices, environmental or social impact, and regulatory and reputational risks.

As museums venture into the arena of ESG investing, many organizations start with simple statements that outline such interests in broad terms. The Maryhill Museum of Art, profiled in this chapter, notes in its investment policy that investments are to be made in funds "of like character and with like aims," designed to ensure that the museum invests in funds that are financially risk averse and compliant with ethics.[16]

Across the nonprofit field, mission relevance is playing an increasingly large role in investing activities and financial transparency. As your organization considers if and how to incorporate such an initiative, there are resources available to assist you. Some investment managers who manage nonprofit clients are familiar with MRI/ESG investing and may be able to provide guidance. For more general information, there are websites that provide information, such as Cambridge Associates, a global investment firm that produces content on investment approaches and the Upstart Co-Lab, which promotes impact investing in the cultural sector.

* * * * *

CASE STUDY: WALTERS ART MUSEUM
BALTIMORE, MARYLAND

Mission: The mission of the Walters Art Museum is to bring art and people together for enjoyment, discovery, and learning. We create a place where people of every

Figure 5.3. Walters Art Museum. Courtesy of the Walters Art Museum.

background can be touched by art. We engage and strengthen our community by collecting, preserving, and interpreting art."

Founded as the Walters Art Gallery in 1934, the Walters Art Museum was established with a gift bequeathed to the City of Baltimore by Atlantic Coast Line Railroad president Henry Walters.[17] Like his father, William Walters, Henry Walters was an art collector. His collection included classical and Western medieval objects, European painting, and, most notably, the entire contents of the Palazzo Accoramboni in Rome, which he acquired in 1902. Walters's gift to the City of Baltimore included 22,000 objects, two buildings, and an endowment, all designated to serve "the benefit of the public."[18]

Today, the Walters Art Museum functions on an annual operating budget of $15 million, with approximately 150 full-time staff members. The museum functions as a "quasi City agency" and maintains formal partnerships with both the State of Maryland and the City of Baltimore, which has been a positive relationship: in 2006, for instance, the museum was able to abolish admissions fees through a city grant program. The museum does maintain a governing board of approximately 35 members, and on which sits the mayor of Baltimore and the president of the city council in ex officio positions. Director Julia Marciari-Alexander, who has served in her role since 2013, notes that the board serves as a working board; much of their oversight is conducted via committee service and brought to the full board for review.[19]

The museum consists of five buildings, three of which are owned by the City of Baltimore, along with Walters's original bequest of 22,000 objects. The property includes the Palazzo Building, constructed in 1909 and modeled after a seventeenth-century Italian palace to house the original collection; the Centre Street Building, which dates to 1974 and includes exhibition spaces, an auditorium, café, and gift shop; and 1 West Mount Vernon Place, also known as the Hackerman House, a nineteenth-century preserved townhouse that functions as an experimental installation space. The holdings of the museum consist of two additional buildings used for administrative needs and a collection that has grown to approximately 36,000 objects, representative of a variety of cultures, art historical periods, and geography.[20]

Since its founding in 1934, the museum has prioritized its focus on community and representation. The name change to the Walters Art Museum, in 2000, was designed to showcase the institutional standing in Baltimore and its role as a cultural center. Under Marciari-Alexander's leadership, the museum has magnified its concentration on issues of representation in new ways. According to the museum website, "while previous descriptions of William and Henry Walters have focused on their roles as philanthropists and art collectors, the Museum is now addressing and examining their support of the Confederacy and their Eurocentric collecting."[21] In addition to the language addressing their founding, the Walters Art Museum website also includes a draft land acknowledgment regarding the original settlement of Indigenous populations and scholarly references to educate the public.

In addition to its public messaging and content, the Walters Art Museum's focus on transparency extends to its financial management. The endowment of the museum was established as part of the original bequest made by Henry Walters in 1931 and to support the transition of the museum from a publicly accessible private exhibition space to its opening as a public institution in 1934. When Marciari-Alexander joined the museum in 2013, the endowment was valued at $110 million, of which an annual draw of 4.8 percent supported a $3.8 million operating budget.[22] A 2008 through 2015 endowment campaign raised $30 million, especially notable since the 2009 recession pressured many other organizations to reduce fundraising activities.

The year 2015 was pivotal in the management of the endowment and marked the advent of the Museum's diverse manager strategy: ten percent of the museum's endowment was invested with firms owned by women and people of color as a commitment to diversity, equity, accessibility, and inclusion (DEAI) and in alignment with the institutional strategic plan. The annual draw was increased to 5 percent to accommodate the diversity initiative and capital maintenance; the shift allowed for the museum to meet these needs while still prioritizing the conservation of the endowment principal. Marciari-Alexander notes that the strength of the board, and particularly the shared expertise of the investment committee, allowed for such an ideological shift in the investment strategy and its reflection of the alignment between the museum and the City of Baltimore.

In the years since, the Walters Art Museum has received acclaim for its diversity strategy.[23] The endowment of the Walters Art Museum is now valued at approximately $200 million, which consists of unrestricted funds to support general operations, as well as funds particular to endowed positions, publications, and exhibitions. Almost 50 percent of the $15 million budget is from endowment income. Today, 21 percent of the endowment is invested with minority- and women-owned funds. The museum has created the Socially Responsible Investing Subcommittee, which liaises with both a DEAI staff-board working group and a DEAI board committee. Looking ahead, Marciari-Alexander expects to focus on impact investing, with a $2 million investment from the endowment in Baltimore organizations, while continuing endowment growth to fund collections, staff development and equitable compensation, capital needs, and DEAI priorities. In reference to the planned impact investing strategy, Marciari-Alexander notes: "When Baltimore succeeds, so do we."

What Can We Learn?

- *Synthesize fundraising objectives with institutional vision.* By marrying the priority of endowment growth with its strategic plan, the Walters Art Museum has ensured transparency in multiple aspects of its operation and a practicable plan for future institutional growth.
- *The value of the message and investment returns can be mutually beneficial.* The Walters Art Museum's recrafting its narrative to embrace its Baltimore community and ongoing partnership with the city has served to strengthen both its regional ties and its ESG-centered investments.

★ ★ ★ ★ ★

ISSUES IN THE FIELD: GOVERNING BOARDS AND FINANCIAL HEALTH

In a 2021 article for *Hyperallergic*, provocatively titled "The Financial Reasons for Abolishing Boards," artist and writer Clark Filio posited that nonprofit endowments are not only poorly managed by their board members but actually endangered by their oversight.[24] Citing the Whitney Museum of American Art as an example, Filio explains that the financial returns on many museum endowments are lower than they should be, and trustees charged with managing the funds and the relationships with investment managers may not adequately fulfil their responsibilities. Filio states that such funds are "particularly vulnerable to predatory sales pitches from fund managers looking to hock risky and hard to understand financial products . . . after all, it's not [the trustees'] money they're risking."

Filio admits he is a novice in understanding institutional finance, but his piece speaks to an issue that has received consistent attention in our collective understanding of museums and how they are governed. Board members are charged with the governance of the institution and oversight of resources, inclusive of endowments. While Filio's article certainly raises valuable questions about the role of board members and their ability to act in good faith on behalf of the organization, particularly in relation to financial oversight, most organizations benefit from the expertise that trustees and investment committee members can offer. The Whitney example cited by Filio is worthy of discussion, though by no means representative of the vast majority of institutional endowments, many of which are relatively small in size in the investment world. In fact, nonprofit institutions have more direct ties to the community than their for-profit peers, and board members have mandates to act in good faith in representing the organization in business matters—and often feel a personal allegiance to the institution and its healthy future. In addition to the fact that the typical museum endowment is not the size to be an attractive target to predatory tactics—nor would it serve the public representation of firms and trustees looking to manipulate nonprofit financial health—sites without massive endowments tend to be risk-averse, rely on more conservative approaches to endowment management, and realize better and more consistent returns with relatively modest investing power.

The conversation about abolishing boards? That will wait for another day. As long as the trustees are acting in good faith in their governance of institutional assets, including the endowment, we are working toward the shared goal of financial sustainability.

★ ★ ★ ★ ★

CONCLUSION

As this chapter shows, the concept of the public trust is rapidly evolving. Where once the focus was on compliance with accounting standards and the classification of museums as nonprofit entities, now the role of transparency encompasses so much more. The expectation of financial acuity is not simply to ensure the existence of museums, but in their ability to thrive as cultural epicenters and in the service of social justice, equity, and representation in both internal and external activities. This responsibility extends beyond conventional readings of the educational value of exhibitions and programs that, to be sure, play an essential role in the public value of museums. Yet museum accountability now extends to organizational health and holdings, both collections and financial assets, including where and with whom funds are invested. Such expectations signal a shift in the public perception of museums from gatekeepers to knowledge and documentarians of the past to agents of social and even economic change.

Between 2018 and 2020, one-third of *all* assets under professional management in the United States were invested in impact investing strategies, documenting a whopping 42 percent increase in just two years.[25] As the impetus grows to invest with the goal of societal impact and not just to maximize financial returns, mission-based organizations are charged to put their money where their mouths are, so to speak. The evolution in our understanding of financial transparency and the increasing institutional embrace of social issues indicates that the financial, physical, and cultural position that museums hold mandates their accountability for transparency at all levels.

Key Points: What Have We Learned?

- Transparency is indispensable in helping donors, staff, trustees, and the general community understand the financial mechanisms and compliant practices, but also in their comprehension of institutional goals and vision.
- Endowments can be undervalued as an internal financial process and without direct public benefit; here, we see that endowment management itself can serve the mission and even function as a form of mission execution and community engagement.

NOTES

1. Often, 990 returns are reproduced in full-on websites such as Guidestar.org and CharityNavigator.org. If an organization's return includes donor-identifying information like home addresses, such information is redacted from public view.
2. Colleen Schafroth, interview with the Rebekah Beaulieu, June 10, 2021.
3. Colleen Schafroth, interview with the Rebekah Beaulieu, June 10, 2021.
4. "Socially Responsible Investment Guidelines," United States Conference of Catholic Bishops, November 12, 2003, https://www.usccb.org/about/financial-reporting/socially-responsible-investment-guidelines.
5. "Socially Responsible Investment Guidelines," United States Conference of Catholic Bishops.
6. "The Database of Fossil Fuel Divestment Commitments Made by Institutions Worldwide," Global Fossil Fuel Divestment Commitments Database, https://gofossilfree.org/divestment/commitments/.
7. "The Database of Fossil Fuel Divestment Commitments Made by Institutions Worldwide," Global Fossil Fuel Divestment Commitments Database.
8. "Ford Foundation Commits $1 Billion from Endowment to Mission-Related Investments," Ford Foundation, April 5, 2017, https://www.fordfoundation.org/the-latest/news/ford-foundation-commits-1-billion-from-endowment-to-mission-related-investments/.
9. "Ford Foundation Commits $1 Billion from Endowment to Mission-Related Investments," Ford Foundation.
10. Valentina Di Liscia, "Can Museums Use Their Endowments to Support the Greater Good?" *Hyperallergic*, December 2, 2020, https://hyperallergic.com/604770/can-museums-use-their-endowments-to-support-the-greater-good/.
11. Laura Callahan, "Museums should lead in socially responsible investing," *Financial Times*, September 2, 2019, https://www.ft.com/content/b7328400-c432-11e9-ae6e-a26d1d0455f4/.

12. Anna Raginskaya, "Sustainable Investing—A Practical Guide for Museums (Part 1)," *Center for the Future of Museums* (blog), December 1, 2019, https://www.aam-us.org/2019/12/01/sustainable-investing-a-practical-guide-for-museums-part-1/.

13. Raginskaya, "Sustainable Investing (Part 1)."

14. Anna Raginskaya, "Sustainable Investing—A Practical Guide for Museums (Part 2)," *Center for the Future of Museums* (blog), December 9, 2019, https://www.aam-us.org/2019/12/09/sustainable-investing-a-practical-guide-for-museums-part-2/.

15. Intentional Endowments, "Samples of Investment Policy Language," *Intentional Endowments*, September 3, 2021, https://d3n8a8pro7vhmx.cloudfront.net/intentionalendowments/pages/2866/attachments/original/1539283280/SampleIPSlanguage-ESG.pdf?1539283280.

16. "Statement of Investment Policy, Objectives and Guidelines for Maryhill Museum of Art Funds," Maryhill Museum of Art, November 21, 2019, http://www.maryhillmuseum.org/2013/wp-content/uploads/2013/02/InvestmentPolicy_rev20100128.pdf.

17. "About the Walters: Past, Present, Future," Walters Art Museum, last updated March 2021, https://thewalters.org/about/.

18. "About the Walters," Walters Art Museum.

19. Julia Marciari-Alexander, interview with the Rebekah Beaulieu, June 23, 2021.

20. Ibid.

21. "About the Walters," Walters Art Museum.

22. Julia Marciari-Alexander, interview with the Rebekah Beaulieu, June 23, 2021.

23. Laura Callanan, "How Museums Can Ethically Invest Their Money," *The Art Newspaper*, March 30, 2021, https://www.theartnewspaper.com/comment/how-museums-can-ethically-invest-their-money.

24. Clark Filio, "The Financial Reasons for Abolishing Boards," *Hyperallergic*, June 6, 2021, https://hyperallergic.com/651099/the-financial-reasons-for-abolishing-museum-boards/.

25. Elizabeth Merritt, "Investing for Values and Mission," *Center for the Future of Museums* (blog), March 23, 2021, https://www.aam-us.org/2021/03/23/investing-for-values-and-mission/.

6

Final Thoughts

In recent years, there has been an increased interest in the financial sustainability in museums. From the pledge of national organizations such as the American Alliance of Museums (AAM) to address financial sustainability as part of their core functions in 2019, to the acuity of virtually all museums in the United States in response to the COVID pandemic in 2020, sound financial management and viability is inarguably central to the future of museums. Financial sustainability can seem inscrutable and hard to attain for organizations that are small, without resources to spare or experts to offer guidance, as well as those that are large, complex sites that require intensive management. The pressure to find a path to sustainability is indeed a challenge, especially as the expectations for museums extend from traditional requirements of contribution management and compliance to now include to mission relevance and nuanced investment oversight.

In a 2016 article, then president of AAM, Ford Bell, cited a notable figure: over half of American museums reported suffering moderate to severe financial stress.[1] The momentous cultural change marked the COVID-19 pandemic, as well as ongoing social justice initiatives, creates a climate in which all functions of a museum are beholden to their mission and value as community anchors. In order for museums to maintain their vital role as civic agents, they are increasingly responsible for transparent and progressive financial activities that serve their educational missions and are held to the high standards of the public trust.

Museums are evolving their income streams to embrace a broad system of earned income and contributions, amass more diversified asset holdings, and consider financial vitality as a core profit of nonprofit management. Sound financial systems and consistent oversight are essential elements of financial sustainability, and endowments can serve a key role in their ability to support regular operating needs, special projects, and to weather unforeseen circumstances.

These chapters have attended to a variety of topics both integral to understanding museums as well as issues in the field. Chapter 1 introduced endowment terminology, functions, and forms, and weighed the decision organizations face when considering whether or not to establish a new endowment. Chapter 2 addressed the role of board governance and financial oversight responsibilities, as well as the role of institutional development in endowment planning. In the third chapter, topics included accounting needs and fund management, and considerations of endowment usage and overspending. Chapter 4 detailed fundraising administration and donor communications regarding endowments, and explained some of the common misassumptions surrounding endowment use and availability of funds. The final chapter focused on transparency and mission relevance, with particular attention to the role of boards and financial health. My hope is that this is only an early entry into a growing canon of resources dedicated to long-term financial planning to offer everyone in our field—not just the financial whiz on the board, or the CPA that provides bookkeeping services—to contribute to meaningful discussions of finance, resource management, and institutional planning.

It is plain to see that a commitment to financial health is essential to healthy and relevant organizations. For many museums, this includes strong endowment management. The arbitrary chasm is closing between programmatic interests that are reflective of mission and business administration that is not mission dependent. Endowments are a character in the narrative of the institution—including its mission engagement—and not simply to serve the purpose of financial returns.

Unlike other financial activities of a nonprofit institution, the endowment holds a unique position in its support of the future of an organization, its ability to evolve, to grow in scale and scope. Endowments are avenues to intergenerational equity, and their service to an organization is continually relevant. In this text, we have discussed how to build a sound policy, to manage gifts and donor communications, and to properly process funds through development and business offices. In addition to the infrastructural elements of endowments, we have also raised the central tenet of the endowment: the building of legacy. The word *legacy* is something we often mention to donors, or as we invite visitors to become members. But how often do we reflect on what we are saying? We are working together to build institutions that will not only exist for generations to come. They are also laboratories of learning inspiration, and community of which we can be proud, while continually striving to make them the best they can be.

Those of us who serve museums as staff, trustees, or volunteers recognize that the mission we serve benefits the communities of today as well as those to come. When we invest in the strong financial management of these sites, we invest in their future.

Invest wisely.

NOTE

1.	Ford W. Bell, "How Are Museums Supported Financially in the US?" United States Department of State Bureau of International Information Programs, 2016, https://publications.america.gov/wp-content/uploads/sites/8/2016/03/You-Asked-Series_How-Are-Museums-Supported-Financially-in-the-US_English_Lo-Res_508.pdf.

Glossary of Terms

active investing: An investment strategy that involves ongoing buying and selling based on market conditions to reach maximum profitability.

articles of incorporation: The formal declaration of organization. Also referred to as "articles of association," "certificate of association," or a similar name determined by state.

business plan: The "who and what" of your operation. This is the functional process by which you expect to accomplish your goals.

bylaws: A document that articulates the rules, policies, and procedures of the organization, particularly in regard to governance.

capital campaign: A targeted fundraising campaign that takes place over a defined period of time, often with the intention to create, preserve, restore, or expand property.

comprehensive campaign: A fundraising campaign that takes place over a defined period of time, inclusive of gifts to capital projects, operational needs, and endowment and other asset growth.

corpus: The amount of the original investment that is to remain untouched in order to allow the monies to accrue value. Also known as the principal.

distribution rate: The calculation by which the annual amount of the appreciated value of a fund is determined.

endowment: An endowment is a donation of money or property that can be sold for monetary value to a nonprofit organization, which uses the income from said gift for a specific purpose. This purpose may be general (unrestricted) or for a defined project or need (restricted). The term endowment can refer to a single fund or donor gift, or a group or number of funds. More colloquially, it typically refers to the totality of a nonprofit institution's investable assets. Endowment funds are invested for a period of time as defined when the endowment is established, typically in perpetuity.

environmental, social, and governance (ESG) investing: A set of criteria by which socially conscious investors consider potential investments according to environmental, social, and governance priorities and activities.

Financial Accounting Standards Board (FASB): The body that sets standards for the implementation of generally accepted accounting principles (GAAP) within the United States.

general endowment: The endowment designed to fund general operational needs.

generally accepted accounting principles (GAAP): The accounting standards set by the United States Securities and Exchange Commission.

gift acceptance policy: The gift acceptance policy is the institution's guidelines for how gifts are accepted and processed. The policy should include language addressing general guidelines that are applicable to all gift transactions, as well as the definition of gift categories and appeals. Procedures for different gift types should be articulated, including those related to cash, stocks and bonds, tangible gifts, or gifts to the collection, such as artwork.

impact investing: Investing made to companies via fund managers to instigate social or environmental impact as well as a financial return on the investment.

investment income: A percentage earned from the investment and available for current use. Also referred to as the distribution or draw.

investment policy: The document guiding institutional investment activities, including but not limited to accountable parties, cash thresholds, and distribution rules and procedures, among other topics.

memorandum of understanding: A document that formalizes the relationship and mutual expectations between a parent organization and a site.

mission statement: A summary statement of the purpose, function, and goals of an organization.

mission-relevant investing (MRI): Investing activity that is aligned with and furthers an organization's mission.

named funds: Funds that are named for a specific donor or to honor an individual, family, or other entity. Also known as honorific funds.

naming agreement: The terms agreed upon by the organization and the donor for funds that are named for a specific donor or to honor an individual, family, or other entity.

passive investing: A long-term strategy in which investors hold a diversified portfolio with the goal of reaching market standing.

pledge agreement: Common for those giving to capital campaigns, comprehensive campaigns, or a large amount according to a schedule, the pledge agreement allows for installments to be made toward a stated amount over a period of time. The typical pledge agreement includes total donation amount, the date and terms of the gift agreement, and the anticipated payment installment schedule.

principal: The amount of the original investment that is to remain untouched in order to allow the monies to accrue value. Also known as the corpus.

quasi endowments: Funds that do not have an external restriction and are used according to the discretion of the governing board of trustees, whether according to a particular schedule or for a specific use. They are also called board-restricted funds.

reserve funds: Funds that are available and ready for use. Their high liquidity makes them ideal for accommodating cash flow issues or to fund capital needs, technological upgrades, unforeseen expenses, or other costs that exceed budget expectations but are necessary expenditures.

restricted funds: Funds that carry donor restrictions, which may explicate guidelines according to use, timeline, and capacity.

securities gifts: A form of a noncash contribution, usually of appreciated stock or mutual funds.

specific use funds: Funds that are restricted for particular use, typically mission-direct activities such as educational programs, acquisitions, exhibition, or conservation of the collection.

spending policy: A usage structure determined by a board to ensure that the growth of the fund's assets will meet or exceed inflation over time.

statement of cash flows: The financial document that accounts for the change in cash and cash equivalents during a financial period, and summarizes the sources and uses of cash during the corresponding period of the statement of activity.

statement of financial activity: The document of the income and the expenditures of an organization and how they relate to each other. Also called an income statement or a profit and loss statement (P&L).

statement of financial position: A comprehensive record of organizational financial standing. Also called a balance sheet.

statement of functional expenses: The documentation of organizational expenses by functional area, typically designated into programming and administrative categorizations.

strategic plan: The "how and when" of your organization, including operation, its priorities, and goals.

term endowment funds: Funds that are restricted by the timeframe of their existence, whether defined by a particular period of time or upon the occurrence of a specific event.

total return: The return on an investment inclusive of market gains or losses and income from interest, dividends, or rental payments.

transparency: The ability and willingness of an organization to disclose financial information in a timely and compliant manner.

true endowment. A fund that can be limited in time or be held in perpetuity and used to fund general operations or a specific purpose.

unrestricted funds: Funds that are not beholden to any external restriction regarding use or purpose.

Index

specific-use funds, 5–6; spending policy, 23, 38, 123; structures of, 3–4, 10, 17; term endowments, 6, 123; true endowments, 6, 30, 124. See also board of directors

environmental, social, and governance (ESG) investing, 49, 105–112; definition of, 121. See also mission relevant investing (MRI)

ESG investing. See environmental, social, and governance (ESG) investing

Financial Accounting Standards Board (FASB), 43, 99; definition of, 122

financial reporting, 18–20, 22–23, 29, 37–38, 43, 89, 97–100; annual report, 29, 43, 97–100

Form 990. See IRS form 990

fundraising, 2, 9, 57–60, 77, 81–83, 84, 88–91, 92–94; and stewardship reporting, 19, 37. See also endowments

generally accepted accounting principles (GAAP), 98; definition of, 122. See also Financial Accounting Standards Board

gift acceptance policies, 60, 60–76; definition of, 122

impact investing. See environmental, social, and governance (ESG) investing

institutional documentation, 18–19

Internal Revenue Code 501(c)(3), 13, 54, 91

investment committee, 22–23, 29–30, 32, 38, 48, 84; charter 22–23, 24–28

investment policy, 23, 29–32, 91, 102, 106–9, definition of, 122

IRS form 990, 97–100, 114n1

J. F. Slater Memorial Museum (Norwich, Connecticut): audit of, 12; case study of, 10–13; endowment, 12; mission statement of, 10; and Norwich Free Academy, 12; restricted and unrestricted funds, 12

Los Angeles County Museum of Art (Los Angeles, California): case study of, 20–22; endowment, 21–22; mission statement of, 20; restricted funds, 22

Maryhill Museum of Art (Goldendale, Washington): case study of, 100-2; endowment, 101–2; Endowment, Reserves and Funds Policy, 103-4; investment policy, 102, 109; mission statement of, 100; and transparency, 102

memorandum of understanding, 33; definition of, 122. See also parent organization

mission relevant investing (MRI), 105–9; definition of, 122. See also environmental, social, and governance (ESG) investing

mission statement, 18–19; definition of, 122. See also institutional documentation

named funds. See endowments

naming agreements. See endowments

Natural History Museum of Utah (Salt Lake City, Utah): annual endowment distribution of, 34; case statement of, 80, 81; case study of, 33–34; endowment, 34; endowment campaign, 80; mission statement of, 33. See also parent organization

operating budget, 20, 29, 38–39, 51–52, 55, 81, 91–93, 110–11

parent organization, 12–13, 38. See also memorandum of understanding

planned giving, 2, 33, 43, 49, 83–84, 88; charitable trusts, 3, 84. See also bequests

pledge agreements, 53, 75; definition of, 122

principal, 3–4, 7, 10, 30–32, 38, 42, 46, 53–55, 99, 102, 111; definition of, 123. See also endowments

quasi endowments. *See* board of directors

restricted funds, 1, 4-6, 12, 14n5, 20-22, 33, 39, 42-43, 51, 53-55, 57-59, 77, 83-84, 99, 101-2, 121; definition of, 123. *See also* endowments

Rotch-Jones Duff House and Garden Museum (New Bedford, Massachusetts): case study of, 7-9; endowment, 7-9; mission statement of, 7

spending policy. *See* endowments

statement of nonprofit tax exemption, 18. *See also* institutional documentation

strategic plan, 19, 33, 43, 59, 111-12; definition of, 123. *See also* institutional documentation

Strawbery Banke Museum (Portsmouth, New Hampshire): and active fund management, 84; capital campaign, 84, 88, *85-87*; case study of, 83-88; and crisis management, 84, 88; endowment, 84-88; mission statement of, 83; restricted and unrestricted funding, 84

transparency, 32-33, 35, 46-47, 59, 83, 97-102, 109, 111-14, 117-18, 124

trustees. *See* board of directors

unrestricted funds 1, 4, 6, 12, 17, 21, 23, 33, 39, 46, 48, 52-53, 55, 59, 83, 99, 112, 121; definition of, 124. *See also* endowments

vision statement, 19. *See also* institutional documentation

Walters Art Museum (Baltimore, Maryland): case study of, 109-12; and diversity, equity, accessibility, and inclusion (DEAI), 111-12; endowment, 110-12; and environmental, social, and governance (ESG) investments, 111-12; mission statement of, 109-10; and transparency, 111-12

Woodlawn Museum (Ellsworth, Maine): capital campaigns, 46; case study of, 45-47; endowment, 46-47; financial policies of, 46-47; mission statement of, 45

About the Author

Rebekah Beaulieu PhD has been a museum professional for over twenty years. She currently serves as the director of the Florence Griswold Museum, a 12-acre National Historic Landmark historic house, art museum, and interpreted landscape in Old Lyme, Connecticut. Becky previously served as the director of the Winchester Historical Society in Winchester, Massachusetts, and as the associate director of the Bowdoin College Museum of Art in Brunswick, Maine.

Becky serves as an accreditation commissioner for the American Alliance of Museums and as treasurer of the American Association of State and Local History. In 2022, she was appointed editor of the AASLH book series.

In addition to her professional work, Becky is adjunct assistant professor of art history at Connecticut College in New London, Connecticut. She teaches professional development courses for the Society of American Archivists and the American Association of State and Local History, and has guest lectured at Fairfield University, George Washington University, and Boston University.

Becky is also co-editor of The State of Museums: Voices from the Field (MuseumsEtc., 2019) and the author of Financial Fundamentals for Historic House Museums (Rowman & Littlefield, 2017). She holds an MA in art history and museum studies from the University of Wisconsin-Milwaukee, an MA in arts administration from Columbia University, and a PhD in American and New England studies from Boston University. She lives in Old Saybrook, Connecticut, with her husband and three very pampered cats.

To contact Becky, please visit www.rebekah.beaulieu.com.